Dawn of the Messiah

THE COMING OF CHRIST
IN SCRIPTURE

Edward Sri

SERVANT
BOOKS

PUBLISHED BY ST. ANTHONY MESSENGER PRESS
CINCINNATI, OHIO

RESCRIPT

In accord with the *Code of Canon Law*, I hereby grant my permission to publish *Dawn of the Messiah: The Coming of Christ in Scripture*, by Edward Sri.

Archbishop Joseph F. Naumann
Archdiocese of Kansas City, Kansas

The permission to publish is a declaration that a book or pamphlet is considered to be free from doctrinal or moral error. It is not implied that those who have granted the permission to publish agree with the contents, opinions or statements expressed.

Cover design by Cindy Dunne

Cover image: Angelico, Fra (1387-1455), Presentation of Jesus in the Temple. Fresco. Museo di S. Marco, Florence, Italy. © Scala/Art Resource, NY.

Book design by Phillips Robinette, O.F.M.

Library of Congress Cataloging-in-Publication Data

Sri, Edward P.
  Dawn of the Messiah : the coming of Christ in Scripture / Edward Sri.
      p. cm.
  Includes bibliographical references.
  ISBN 0-86716-720-3 (pbk. : alk. paper)
  1. Jesus Christ—Birth. I. Title.
  BT315.3.S74 2005
  232.92—dc22

2005002657

ISBN 0-86716-720-3

Published by Servant Books, an imprint of St. Anthony Messenger Press
28 W. Liberty St.
Cincinnati, OH 45202
www.AmericanCatholic.org

Printed in the United States of America.

Printed on acid-free paper.

05 06 07 08 09 5 4 3 2 1

Contents

Dedicated with love and prayers
to my daughter, Madeleine
and my son, Paul.

May the wonder and joy you have now in
the mystery of Christ's birth
fill your hearts with his love all the days of your lives.

Isaiah 9:6
Matthew 2:10-11

ACKNOWLEDGMENTS

I am grateful to Curtis Mitch for his friendship and his always valuable counsel and feedback. I also thank the many people who have been a part of this work through their prayers and exploration with me into the Gospel accounts of Christ's birth, especially my students and colleagues at Benedictine College and in FOCUS and the sisters in the Midwest region of the Missionaries of Charity. Most of all, I thank my wife Elizabeth not only for her support and encouragement for this project, but also for filling our family life at home with the true spirit of Advent and Christmas each year. I cannot think of a better environment in which to have reflected on the mystery of Christ's coming while writing and editing much of this book.

"The Hopes and Fears of All the Years…"

P ERHAPS THE CHRISTMAS STORY has become almost *too* familiar.

Every December we encounter the story of Christ's birth in manger scenes, Christmas cards and decorations on Christmas trees. We hear it in the Scriptures, sing it in the carols and see it in the paintings, statues and stained-glass windows that decorate our churches. For many today the basic outline of this narrative has become so familiar that the profound—indeed, shocking—nature of the Christmas mystery might be overlooked. The tale of a virgin giving birth, a child laid in a manger and shepherds greeted by angels no longer arrests our attention. It all seems part of the same ordinary story we have heard countless times since childhood.

But what if we had never heard the story before? What if we were Jews in the first century who were hearing this plot for the first time? What would these Christmas stories in the Bible mean to us? These events at the dawn of Christianity certainly would not have been taken for granted. They would have signaled to us that everything our nation had been longing for, for hundreds of years, was now coming to fulfillment.

The Catholic Church's Midnight Mass liturgy for Christmas Eve reminds us of how earthshaking this story was originally. At a dramatic moment in the opening of the Mass, the following proclamation is often made to remind us that Christ's birth in Bethlehem really is the turning point of the history of the world:

> Today, the twenty-fifth day of December,
> unknown ages from the time
> when God created the heavens and the earth
> and then formed man and woman in his own image.
>
> Several thousand years after the flood,
> when God made the rainbow shine forth
> as a sign of the covenant.
>
> Twenty-one centuries from the time of Abraham and Sarah;
> thirteen centuries after Moses led the people of Israel out of Egypt.
>
> Eleven hundred years from the time of Ruth and the Judges;
> one thousand years from the anointing of David as king;
> in the sixty-fifth week according to the prophecy of Daniel.
>
> In the one hundred and ninety-fourth Olympiad;
> the seven hundred and fifty-second year from the foundation of the city of Rome.
>
> The forty-second year of the reign of Octavian Augustus;
> the whole world being at peace,
> Jesus Christ, eternal God and Son of the eternal Father,
> desiring to sanctify the world by his most merciful coming,
> being conceived by the Holy Spirit,
> and nine months having passed since his conception,
> was born in Bethlehem of Judea of the Virgin Mary.
> Today is the nativity of our Lord Jesus Christ,
> according to the flesh.[1]

The point of this proclamation is clear. From the creation of man and woman at the beginning of time all the way up to the reign of the Roman Empire in the first century, the story of the human family reaches its climax in the coming of this child. Bethlehem thus becomes the stage for the final act of God's saving plan. The Christmas hymn "O, Little Town of Bethlehem" hits it right on the mark when it says, "The hopes and fears of all the years are met in thee tonight."

Back to Bethlehem

Interestingly, the Bible does not offer a lot of information about the birth of the Messiah. In fact, only two Gospels—Matthew and Luke—give us any of the details. And these provide us with merely a glimpse of Christ's birth and childhood, devoting only a total of four chapters to this part of his life.

Yet these are four powerful chapters overflowing with allusions to Old Testament stories and prophecies of great hope. These narratives would have triggered in people's minds various expectations from the Jewish tradition about the great things God would do one day for Israel and for the whole world. By drawing on these hopes, the Gospel accounts of Christ's birth proclaim that God's plan for all of humanity was coming to fruition in this child.

The profound meaning of these stories is often lost to modern readers who are not familiar with the Jewish Scriptures, prophecies and historical settings that shaped the worldview of people in Jesus' day. The goal of this book is to help bring the reader back into the first-century Jewish world so as to discover many of the spiritual treasures that are packed into practically every line and every detail of these Gospel accounts.

Take, for example, the story of the Magi who follow a star in search of a king (see Matthew 2:1-11). For many Christians today, this might appear to be simply a story about gentiles who travel a long way to bring gifts to Jesus. However, for Jews in the first century, the account would have stirred up hopes surrounding the royal prophecy of Numbers 24:17-19. There it was foretold that one day a great king would come to Israel and defeat its enemies. Further, the sign of a great star in the sky would accompany his birth. By including the Magi story in his Gospel with these echoes of Numbers 24, Matthew intends to show us that this prophecy is coming to fulfillment in the child Jesus. The great king of Israel is finally here.

Or consider the words that the angel Gabriel used to greet Mary at the Annunciation: "The Lord is with you" (Luke 1:28). For many Catholics today, this phrase probably brings to mind what the priest says throughout the Mass. However, in the Old Testament these words were used by angels, and even by God himself, to address someone who was being set apart for a special purpose in God's saving plan. The greeting would have signaled to Mary that God was calling her to a daunting mission, one with many risks and trials. Being aware of this background helps modern readers to appreciate the intense vocation Mary was given at the Annunciation. We also can better appreciate her complete self-surrender in accepting this calling.

Enter the Mystery

These are just two simple examples of how understanding the original context can enrich our reading of the Christmas story. By returning to that first-century Jewish setting, we can discover the profound meaning these stories would have had for the first

Christians. And in so doing, it is my hope that we also will be able to understand more clearly the importance the Christmas story continues to have for our lives today.

This book focuses on the two Gospels that offer accounts of the coming of the Messiah: Luke and Matthew. We start with Luke's presentation (Luke 1–2) because it offers the big picture of the events surrounding Christ's birth. Luke begins with the angel Gabriel announcing the birth of Christ's forerunner, John the Baptist. He then covers Christ's own conception in the Annunciation to Mary and the meeting of the two children while in their mothers' wombs in the visitation scene. After telling about the birth and naming of John, Luke focuses on Christ's birth and presentation in the temple. He concludes his second chapter with Jesus as a twelve-year-old boy lost and found in Jerusalem.

Then we will consider the particular narratives about the birth of the Messiah in Matthew's Gospel (chapters. 1 and 2): the royal genealogy of Jesus, Joseph's dilemma about what to do with Mary, the coming of the Magi, and the Holy Family's flight to Egypt.

The commentary that follows draws on contemporary biblical scholarship as well as insights from Catholic tradition. This is intended to be a practical, easy-to-read book that will be helpful for a wide range of people. Reflection questions at the end of each chapter can be used for small group Bible study or personal devotion. It is my hope that priests and religious, catechists and laypeople will find in these pages insights that will help them enter more deeply into the mystery of Christ's coming in Scripture.

CHAPTER ONE

A New Era Dawning
The Annunciation to Zechariah
(Luke 1:5-25)

> In the days of Herod, king of Judea, there was a priest named Zechariah, of the division of Abijah; and he had a wife of the daughters of Aaron, and her name was Elizabeth. And they were both righteous before God, walking in all the commandments and ordinances of the Lord blameless. But they had no child, because Elizabeth was barren, and both were advanced in years.
>
> —LUKE 1:5-7

IT HAS BEEN SAID that Luke begins his Gospel like a good Shakespearean play: with a pair of minor characters who prepare the way for the lead roles to take the stage.[1] Before the main drama surrounding Joseph, Mary and Jesus begins, this first scene in the Gospel of Luke introduces us to an important supporting cast: Zechariah and Elizabeth, an older Jewish couple who are about to be caught up into God's plan of salvation in a way they probably never imagined.

Waiting for a Child

Zechariah and Elizabeth stand out as a couple with high credentials in first-century Judaism. Members of the priesthood were honored among the Jews. With Zechariah serving as a priest, and his wife also coming from the priestly family of Aaron, they would hold a position of great respect. Luke, furthermore, goes out of his way to emphasize that they are both "righteous before God" and even "blameless" in following all his commands.

Portrayed thus as a priestly family that is faithful to the Lord, Zechariah and Elizabeth are showcased as model Jews. That is why the next statement in verse 7 would be so shocking to Jewish minds: "But they had no child, because Elizabeth was barren, and both were advanced in years."

Barrenness was often considered shameful in Judaism. It was even seen as evidence of God's punishment (see Deuteronomy 28:15, 18). Yet we know these model Jews are not outside of God's favor. Given the emphasis on their righteousness in the previous verses, this statement in verse 7 introduces us to a tension between their holiness on one hand and their childlessness on the other.

Such a tension brings to mind other godly women of the Old Testament—such as Sarah, Rebekah, Rachel and Hannah—who suffered from barrenness until God miraculously blessed them with a child. Like these great matriarchs of old, Elizabeth waits for God to act in her life. And the reader of Luke's Gospel also waits to see how this tension will be resolved.

Holy Smoke!

> Now while he was serving as priest before God when his division was on duty, according to the custom of the priesthood,

> it fell to him by lot to enter the temple of the Lord and burn
> incense. And the whole multitude of the people were praying
> outside at the hour of incense. And there appeared to him an
> angel of the Lord standing on the right side of the altar of
> incense.
>
> —Luke 1:8-11

Luke now begins to tell us about the day that changed the lives of
Zechariah and Elizabeth forever.

Zechariah serves as a priest in "the division of Abijah," and
his division is on temple duty (see Luke 1:5, 8). With a large
number of priests among the people but only so many duties to
perform in the temple, the priests were divided into twenty-four
groups. Each group would travel to Jerusalem twice a year for a
weeklong rotation of service in the temple and then return home.

When a division reported for its week of service, the priests
cast lots for assignment to duties in the temple. On this particular day Zechariah is chosen to carry out the most treasured task
any priest could hope to perform: "it fell to him by lot to enter the
temple of the Lord and *burn incense*" (Luke 1:9, emphasis added).
In this ritual the priest would represent Israel before God
and pray on behalf of all the people at the morning or evening
sacrifice.

Offering the incense in the temple generally was considered
a once-in-a-lifetime opportunity. After a priest performed this
action, he would not be eligible for the casting of lots for this
privileged duty again. Some priests might go through their whole
careers without ever having the chance to offer the incense.

What made this practice so honorable was not simply the
offering itself but also *the place* where the offering was made—at
the altar of incense. This altar resided in the Holy Place, the

second holiest chamber in the temple, where only priests were allowed to enter.

The altar of incense stood in the rear of the room before a curtain that separated the Holy Place from the innermost sanctuary of the temple, the Holy of Holies. The Holy of Holies is where God's very presence once dwelt over the ark of the covenant. This was truly holy ground, where the Jews believed heaven met earth. Only one priest in Israel—the high priest—could venture past that curtain into the Holy of Holies, and even he could do so only once a year, on the Day of Atonement.

The altar of incense would be the closest to the Holy of Holies that an ordinary priest could ever get. Consequently, for a Levitical priest like Zechariah, being chosen to offer incense meant he had the once-in-a-lifetime chance to pray at that most revered altar and stand just outside the holiest spot on the face of the earth. That is why this would have been one of the greatest days in Zechariah's life. Indeed, it would have represented the pinnacle of his priestly career.

One can imagine Zechariah's approaching the Holy Place, trembling with great awe and wonder as he is about to make an offering at the altar of incense for the first time. One also can imagine his great surprise when he discovers something no other priest has ever seen there before: an angel of the Lord!

Touched by an Angel

And Zechariah was troubled when he saw him, and fear fell upon him. But the angel said to him, "Do not be afraid, Zechariah, for your prayer is heard, and your wife Elizabeth will bear you a son, and you shall call his name John. And you will have joy and gladness, and many will rejoice at his birth; for he will be great before the Lord, and he shall drink no wine

> nor strong drink, and he will be filled with the Holy Spirit,
> even from his mother's womb. And he will turn many of the
> sons of Israel to the Lord their God, and he will go before him
> in the spirit and power of Elijah, to turn the hearts of the
> fathers to the children, and the disobedient to the wisdom of
> the just, to make ready for the Lord a people prepared."
>
> —Luke 1:12-17

Understandably, Zechariah is startled to find an angel beside the altar. The angel quickly assures him not to be afraid and gives him a message from the Lord: his wife Elizabeth will bear a son, and the child should be called John.

What is most interesting about this scene is not simply that Zechariah and Elizabeth finally will be blessed with a child. The angel reveals that this child will bring blessings not only to his parents but to all of the people, for he will be one of the most important prophets ever sent to Israel. Let us consider three amazing things the angel tells Zechariah about this child.

First, he will not consume wine or strong drink. The angel gives this information not to tell us of John's future drinking habits but to indicate that he will be dedicated to the Lord for *special service*. In the Old Testament some Jewish men called "Nazirites" consecrated themselves to God by a vow and separated themselves from normal life. Abstaining from alcohol was a common practice for the Nazirites (see Numbers 6:3; Judges 13:4). So this fact about John indicates that he will be set apart for some special service for the Lord, like a Nazirite.

Second, the angel's description of the child's being "filled with the Holy Spirit, even from the mother's womb" tells us about the kind of service for which John is destined: he will be *a prophet*. It was the Spirit descending on Saul who transformed him into a prophet (see 1 Samuel 10:10), and it was the Spirit of the Lord who spoke through David so that God's word would be upon his tongue (see 2 Samuel 23:2). It was this same Spirit who came upon the prophets Ezekiel, Elijah and Elisha during their ministry in Israel (see Ezekiel 11:5; 2 Kings 2:9-16; see also Joel 2:28). Thus, when the angel says the child will be filled with the Holy Spirit "from his mother's womb," he is presenting John as one of Israel's great prophets, even before he is born.

The New Elijah

Third, the importance of John's prophetic ministry is seen in the final words that the angel uses to describe this child:

> And he will turn many of the sons of Israel to the Lord their God, and he will go before the Lord in the spirit and power of Elijah to turn the hearts of the fathers to the children, and the disobedient to the wisdom of the just, to make ready for the Lord a people prepared.
>
> —LUKE 1:16-17

These verses echo the last prophetic words of the Old Testament. The prophet Malachi announced that the Lord one day would come to redeem Israel, and that he would send his messenger to prepare the people for his arrival. In Malachi 3:1 God said: "Behold, I send my messenger to *prepare* the way before me" (emphasis added). The Book of Malachi goes on to say that this messenger will be like Israel's most famous prophet, Elijah:

> Behold, I will send you *Elijah* the prophet before the great and terrible day of the Lord comes. *And he will turn the hearts of fathers to their children and the hearts of children to their fathers....*
>
> —MALACHI 4:5-6, emphasis added
> (in some translations Malachi 3:23-24)

In light of this Old Testament background, we see that the angel describes John's prophetic ministry as the fulfillment of Malachi's prophecy. John will be the Lord's messenger, the new Elijah, who will prepare the people of Israel for the Lord's coming, which will bring about the reconciliation of families to God and families to each other.

Now we can see that the story of Zechariah and Elizabeth is not simply about a pious Jewish couple suffering from barrenness and God's intervening to bless them with a child. Rather, *their story is representative of the story of Israel.* Just as Zechariah and Elizabeth are barren and hope for God to show favor on them by blessing them with a child, so too are the Jews suffering in the first century and longing for God to show favor on them again by visiting his people, just as Malachi has foretold. God will respond to Zechariah and Elizabeth's desires for a child in a way that answers the needs of *all* the Jewish people: by sending them a son who will prepare the way for the coming of the Lord and the restoration of Israel.

"I Am Gabriel"

And Zechariah said to the angel, "How shall I know this? For I am an old man, and my wife is advanced in years." And the angel answered him, "I am Gabriel, who stand in the presence of God; and I was sent to speak to you, and to bring you this good news. And behold, you will be silent and unable to speak until the day that these things come to pass, because you did not believe my words, which will be fulfilled in their time." And the people were waiting for Zechariah, and they wondered at his delay in the temple. And when he came out, he could not speak to them, and they perceived that he had seen a vision in the temple; and he made signs to them and

remained dumb. And when his time of service was ended, he
went to his home.

—Luke 1:18-23

After hearing all this, Zechariah doubts whether his elderly wife
really will be able to bear a child. He asks the angel: "How shall
I know this? For I am an old man, and my wife is advanced
in years." The angel then gives a mystifying response: "I
am Gabriel…"

Think about that answer. Here the previously anonymous
angel reveals his identity to doubting Zechariah. But how does
this response answer Zechariah's question, "How shall I know
this?" Zechariah did not ask for the angel's name; he asked for
assurances!

Imagine meeting someone on an airplane who advises you
to buy many lottery tickets because you are going to win the lottery sometime this year. Wondering why you should trust this
stranger's advice, you ask him, "How can I believe this will really
happen?" What would you think if the man answered your question simply by giving you his name, "I'm Mr. Smith"? How would
that answer your question?

Avoiding the Question?

Yet the angel Gabriel knew what he was doing. He gave Zechariah
the one bit of information that might help him tie all the pieces
together. This one detail might help Zechariah see that God is
really acting in his very own family's life in order to bring the
story of Israel to its climactic turning point.

Revealing his name was significant because the only time
Gabriel is mentioned in the Old Testament is in the important

visions given to the prophet Daniel. In Daniel 9 the prophet was praying for God to show mercy on his people and bring an end to the Jewish sufferings under foreign oppressors. In the middle of Daniel's prayer, the angel Gabriel appeared to him at the hour of the evening sacrifice—the time when the incense would have been offered in the temple.

In this vision Gabriel delivered a message of good news and bad news to Daniel. On one hand, the people would continue to suffer under pagan nations for a long time to come. On the other hand, at the end of this period of suffering, God would send an anointed prince (the Messiah) to bring an end to sin and atone for iniquity. This anointed one would usher in everlasting righteousness and bring all of Israel's prophecies to fulfillment (see Daniel 9:24-27).

Given this background, we can see Gabriel certainly is no ordinary angel. He is the one who announced the end of Israel's oppression and the beginning of the messianic era to the prophet Daniel. Now this same angel returns for the first time in hundreds of years and appears to Zechariah. Revealing his name—Gabriel—recalls the prophecies of Daniel 9.

The parallels between what happened to Daniel and what just happened to Zechariah highlight this connection even more. Like Daniel, Zechariah *prays on behalf of Israel* as he offers the incense in the temple. Like Daniel, Zechariah makes this prayer *at the hour of the temple sacrifice*. And in the middle of Zechariah's liturgical service, the same angel—*Gabriel*—appears. Luke is clearly inviting his readers to hear the harmony in salvation history and view Zechariah's encounter with the angel in correspondence with Daniel's.[2]

A Silent Retreat

In light of this background, we can see that the angel is revealing much more than his name. And he is announcing to Zechariah much more than the fact that his wife is going to have a child. By saying "I am Gabriel," the angel basically is telling Zechariah that Israel's long period of suffering is ending. Daniel 9 is finally coming to fulfillment, and *Zechariah's own son* is going to play a key part in preparing the people for the long-awaited "anointed one"—the one Gabriel himself originally said would atone for sin, bring everlasting righteousness and fulfill all prophecy!

Indeed, such a profound announcement from an angel would have been enough to leave any pious Jew speechless. However, Zechariah will experience silence for a different reason. Because he doubted the angel, he is left mute. And the punishment seems to fit the crime. Zechariah simply could not believe that his wife would have a child in her old age. Now, as his wife's miraculous pregnancy unfolds before him, Zechariah will have nine months of silence to ponder and reconsider Gabriel's message and to contemplate the profound mission his son will have in God's plan of salvation.

Reflection Questions

1. How are Zechariah and Elizabeth portrayed in Luke 1:5-6? In light of Jewish tradition, why does this make the following verse (Luke 1:7) so surprising?

2. Read Luke 1:9. Why would being chosen to burn incense be such an important moment for Zechariah's priesthood?

3. The angel tells Zechariah three things about his son, John.

   ✳ First, read Luke 1:15a and Numbers 6:1-4. In light of this Old Testament background, what does the angel's statement about John's not drinking alcohol tell us about him?

   ✳ Second, read Luke 1:15b. Consider this statement in light of what happened to the prophets Ezekiel and Elisha (see Ezekiel 11:5 and 2 Kings 2:9-15). What might John's being "filled with the Holy Spirit" tell us about the kind of ministry he will have?

   ✳ Third, read Malachi 4:5-6 (Malachi 3:23-24 in some translations). How does this background shed light on the angel's description of John the Baptist's mission in Luke 1:16-17?

4. How is the story of Zechariah and Elizabeth symbolic of the story of Israel? Do you find in the story any encouragement for your life today?

5. Read Daniel 9:20-23. Notice the parallels between Daniel's experience in these verses and Zechariah's experience in Luke 1.

   ✳ Daniel 9:20: What is Daniel doing when the angel appears?

   ✳ Luke 1:9: What is Zechariah doing when the angel appears?

   ✳ Daniel 9:21: Which angel appears to Daniel?

   ✳ Luke 1:19: Which angel appears to Zechariah?

* Daniel 9:21: At what time does the angel appear to Daniel?

* Luke 1:10: At what time does the angel appear to Zechariah?

* Daniel 9:23: The angel's message is a response to what?

* Luke 1:13: The angel's message is a response to what?

6. In Daniel 9:24 Gabriel foretold that the Jews would endure suffering for a total of "seventy weeks of years." How much time do you think might be meant by "seventy weeks of years"? According to Daniel 9:24, what will happen at the end of this period?

7. In light of this background from Daniel 9, what ancient Jewish hopes would be stirred by the angel Gabriel's appearance to Zechariah?

8. Compare and contrast Zechariah's question in Luke 1:18 with Mary's question in Luke 1:34. Why does Zechariah get punished for his question while Mary does not? Is it okay to question God? If so, how should we do it?

CHAPTER TWO

The Mother of the King
The Annunciation to Mary
(Luke 1:26-38)

> In the sixth month the angel Gabriel was sent from God to a city of Galilee named Nazareth, to a virgin betrothed to a man whose name was Joseph, of the house of David; and the virgin's name was Mary.
>
> —LUKE 1:26-27

WHAT WAS MARY'S LIFE like originally—*before* she learned that she was to become the mother of Israel's Messiah? While Luke's Gospel does not offer a lot of information about the mother of Jesus, it does tell us three important details that allow us to catch a glimpse of Mary's life before the angel Gabriel visited.

First, we learn that she lives in the town of *Nazareth*. This was a small village in the region of Galilee. It was not a famous place, and Jesus' coming from such an obscure village will cause him trouble later in his public ministry. Some will question how he really could be sent from God, since no prophet ever came out of this region (see John 7:52), while others will wonder whether anything good at all could come out of this little town (see John 1:46). Nevertheless, it is precisely here in this humble, insignificant village that God surprisingly calls a young, seemingly ordinary Jewish woman to the extraordinary task of becoming the mother of Israel's king.

Second, Luke describes Mary as *betrothed* to a man by the name of Joseph. In first-century Judaism, betrothal was the first step of a two-stage marriage process. At her betrothal Mary would have consented before public witnesses to marry Joseph, and this would have established the couple as husband and wife. As a *betrothed* wife, however, Mary would have continued to live with her own family, apart from her husband, for up to a year. Only after this period of betrothal would the second stage of marriage take place—the consummation of the marriage and the wife's moving into the husband's home.

Consequently, as a betrothed woman, Mary still would have been living with her family in Nazareth. As such, it makes sense that Luke would describe her at this stage as "a virgin."

Perhaps even more noteworthy, however, is the fact that women in first-century Palestine generally were betrothed in their early teen years. This tells us that Mary probably was a very young woman when God called her to serve as the mother of the Messiah.

The Royal Family

Finally, the most striking point we know about Mary's life prior to the Annunciation is that she married a man from "the house of David" (1:27). This small detail indicates that Mary became part of the most famous family in all of Israel: King David's family.

On one hand, one might expect being a part of the Davidic dynasty to be a great privilege and honor in ancient Jewish culture. After all, it was David who was promised by God an everlasting kingdom (see 2 Samuel 7), and it was David's descendants who ruled God's people for hundreds of years from the throne in Jerusalem (see 1 and 2 Kings). Thus, from a traditional Jewish perspective, Mary is a member not of any ordinary family but of the royal family of David.

On the other hand, David's great dynasty seemed to come to a tragic halt in 586 B.C., when the foreign armies of Babylon invaded Jerusalem, destroyed the temple and carried the Jews away into exile. For most of the six centuries that followed—up to the days of Mary, Joseph and Jesus—one foreign nation after another ruled over the Jews in Palestine. No descendant of David ruled the Jewish people after that devastating blow by Babylon.

In the time of Mary and Joseph, the Jews are suffering under Roman occupation. In such oppressive conditions, being a member of David's family no longer holds the privileges, authority and honor that it held in the glory days of the kings who reigned in Jerusalem. Instead, this Joseph "of the house of David" is a humble carpenter, leading a quiet, ordinary life in the small town of Nazareth.

In sum, the initial portrait of Mary in Luke 1:26-27 is only a vague sketch. She is a young woman, probably in her early teens. She is betrothed to a man with royal Davidic lineage but is living an ordinary life in an insignificant village in Galilee.

"Full of Grace"

> And he came to her and said, "Hail, full of grace, the Lord is with you!" But she was greatly troubled at the saying, and considered in her mind what sort of greeting this might be. And the angel said to her, "Do not be afraid, Mary, for you have found favor with God."
>
> —LUKE 1:28-30

Mary's world radically changes when the angel Gabriel appears to her saying, "Hail, full of grace, the Lord is with you!" Understandably, Mary "was greatly troubled." Imagine being home alone, walking into a room and finding an angel suddenly standing before you! Anyone would be "greatly troubled" by the appearance of a heavenly visitor such as this.

However, Luke's Gospel tells us that Mary is not startled simply by the angel itself but by the angel's *greeting*: "She was greatly troubled *at the saying*, and considered in her mind what sort of *greeting* this might be" (emphasis added).

Why might Mary be so anxious about the angel's words?

First the angel says, "Hail, full of grace." No one else in the Bible has ever been honored by an angel with such an exalted title. The Greek word *kecharitomene*, which here is translated "full of grace," indicates that Mary already possesses God's saving grace. The Lord has prepared her as a pure and holy temple in which the divine Christ child will dwell for nine months. Now the Son of God will reside in the womb of a woman who is full of grace.[1]

The Catholic Church has often turned to this passage when commenting on Mary's Immaculate Conception—the belief that Mary was conceived full of grace as God prepared her to be the mother of the Messiah. As the *Catechism of the Catholic Church* explains:

> To become the mother of the Savior, Mary "was enriched by God with gifts appropriate to such a role." The angel Gabriel at the moment of the annunciation salutes her as "full of grace." In fact, in order for Mary to be able to give the free assent of her faith to the announcement of her vocation, it was necessary that she be wholly borne by God's grace. Through the centuries the Church has become ever more aware that Mary,

"full of grace" through God, was redeemed from the moment of her conception. That is what the dogma of the Immaculate Conception confesses." (#490-491)

"The Lord Is with You!"

Second, the angel says, "The Lord is with you!" Although many Catholics today are accustomed to hearing "The Lord be with you" repeated throughout the Mass, we might not be as familiar with the powerful significance these words originally had in ancient Judaism.

Many times in the Old Testament the words "the Lord is with you" signaled that someone was being called to a daunting task. In fact, these words often accompanied an invitation from God to play a crucial role in his plan of salvation.[2] Such a divine calling generally entailed great sacrifices and challenged people to step out of their comfort zones and put their trust in God like never before.

At the same time, these words offered assurance that they would not face these challenges alone. They would not have to rely solely on their own abilities and talents because God's presence and protection would be with them throughout their mission. Some of Israel's greatest leaders—men like Isaac, Jacob, Joshua, Gideon and David—were told that God would be with them when they were commissioned to serve his people.

One of the most famous stories that illustrates the meaning of "the Lord is with you" can be found in Exodus, when God called Moses at the burning bush to confront Pharaoh and lead the Israelites out of slavery in Egypt. Feeling fearfully inadequate for the job, Moses responded the same way many people respond when they feel they are in over their heads: with a "Why me?"

—and a disbelief that God would call *him* to this important task. Moses said, "*Who am I* that I should go to Pharaoh and bring the sons of Israel out of Egypt?" (Exodus 3:11, emphasis added). Moses worried that he was neither a good enough leader nor a good enough speaker and that the people would not listen to him.

The Lord's response to Moses' fears is striking. God did not say to Moses, "I will send you to a Toastmaster's workshop on public speaking," or, "I'll fly you out to a Franklin-Covey seminar on effective leadership." Rather, God told Moses the one thing he needed to hear most: "*I will be with you*" (Exodus 3:12, emphasis added). God will make up for any of Moses' weaknesses and insecurities, because ultimately Moses' mission is not his own—it is the Lord's.

Similarly, when Mary hears the angel say to her, "The Lord is with you," she is not simply receiving a formal, pious salutation. With these words Mary probably realizes that a lot is being asked of her. She may not know clearly all the challenges that lie ahead, but the words certainly imply that God has a formidable task in store for her. At the same time, the greeting tells her that she will not have to face these difficulties alone. God will give her the one thing she needs most: the assurance that he will be with her.

Favor with God

Third, we learn more of Mary's mission in Luke 1:30, as the angel says, "Do not be afraid, Mary, for you have found favor with God." Like the phrase "The Lord is with you," the notion of finding "favor with God" also would bring to mind a whole roster of Old Testament covenant mediators who were set apart for a special mission in God's plan of salvation.

Noah was the first person in the Bible described as finding favor with God (see Genesis 6:8). God saved him and his family from the flood and gave him a covenant to be the head of a renewed human family. The next person to find favor with God was Abraham (see Genesis 18:2-3). God made a covenant with him, calling on his family to be the instrument through which he would bring blessing to all the nations of the world. Similarly, Moses, the covenant mediator who led Israel out of slavery in Egypt, found favor with God (see Exodus 33:12-17), as did David, for whom God established a kingdom (see 2 Samuel 15:25).

Like these great covenant mediators of the Old Testament, Mary has found favor with God. Walking in the footsteps of Noah, Abraham, Moses and David, Mary now is called to serve as an important cooperator in the divine plan to bring salvation to all the nations.[3]

What Child Is This?

> And behold, you will conceive in your womb and bear a son,
> and you shall call his name Jesus.
> He will be great, and will be called the Son of the Most High;
> and the Lord God will give to him the throne of his father
>   David,
> and he will reign over the house of Jacob for ever;
> and of his kingdom there will be no end.
>
> —LUKE 1:31-33

Now the angel Gabriel gets to the heart of his message and the nature of Mary's mission: Mary will bear a son who will bring Israel's history to its climax. She will be the mother of Israel's long awaited Messiah-King.

Each of these lines is highly charged with Davidic kingdom themes, echoing the covenant promises God made to King David in 2 Samuel 7. Consider the words God spoke to David at the beginning of his kingship in Jerusalem:

> I will make for you a *great* name.... When your days are fulfilled and you lie down with your fathers, I will raise up your offspring after you, who shall come forth from your body, and I will establish his kingdom. He shall build a house for my name, and I will establish *the throne of his kingdom forever. I will be his father, and he shall be my son*...And your house and *your kingdom shall be made sure for ever* before me; *your throne shall be established for ever.*
>
> —2 SAMUEL 7:9, 12-14, 16, emphasis added

We can see numerous parallels between the words God spoke to David and the words Gabriel speaks to Mary. For example, Mary's child is called "son of the Most High," recalling how David's sons were described as having a unique filial-like relationship with God (see 2 Samuel 7:14; Psalm 2:7; 89:26-27). Similarly, God's giving Mary's child "the throne of his father David" brings to mind how David's heir was to receive "the throne of his kingdom for ever" (2 Samuel 7:13). Furthermore, the description of Jesus' never-ending kingdom— "He will reign over the house of Jacob forever; and of his kingdom there will be no end"—reminds us of the everlasting dynasty God originally promised to David's family (see 2 Samuel 7:13, 16; Psalm 89:36-37).

2 Samuel 7	Luke 1
I will make for you a great name (7:9).	He will be great (1:32).
I will be his father, and he shall be my son (7:14).	He...will be called Son of the Most High (1:32).
I will establish the throne of his kingdom for ever (7:13).	And the Lord God will give to him the throne of his father David (1:32)
And your house and your kingdom shall be made sure for ever (7:16).	And he will reign over the house of Jacob for ever, and of his kingdom there will be no end (1:33).

These themes—the throne of David, greatness, sonship, an everlasting kingdom—make the angel's message to Mary quite clear: Mary will have the long awaited royal Son who will fulfill the dynastic promises God made to David.

For hundreds of years the Jews have been longing for God to rebuild the kingdom that Babylon destroyed. Their prophets have foretold that one day God would send a new Davidic heir who would comfort the people in their oppression and free them from their enemies. This new Davidic king not only would restore the great dynasty to its former glory but also would bring Israel's history and the history of the world to its ultimate destination: the reunion of the human family into covenant with God. The Jews called this long-awaited son of David "the anointed one"—or in Hebrew, "the Messiah."

Mary's mission is to be the mother of this particular King, the Messiah. In her womb she is to carry the summation of all of Israel's expectations and the culmination of God's plan of salvation. Indeed, "the hopes and fears of all the years" find their answer in Mary's child.

The Virgin Mother

> And Mary said to the angel, "How shall this be, since I have no husband?" And the angel said to her, "The Holy Spirit will come upon you, and the power of the Most High will overshadow you; therefore the child to be born will be called holy, the Son of God. And behold, your kinswoman Elizabeth in her old age has also conceived a son; and this is the sixth month with her who was called barren. For with God nothing will be impossible." And Mary said, "Behold, I am the handmaid of the Lord; let it be to me according to your word." And the angel departed from her.
>
> —LUKE 1:34-38

It is important to note that up to this point of the angel's announcement, there has been no explicit mention of the child's divine origins. All the language so far about the everlasting kingdom and Jesus' being the Son of God is taken from terms that the Old Testament commonly used to describe the Davidic king.

Also, there has been no explicit mention *yet* of a miraculous virgin birth. Presumably, if Mary were like most first-century betrothed women, she would anticipate conceiving of this child through the natural means of marital relations after her betrothal period ended and after she moved in with her husband.

However, Mary surprisingly asks, "How shall this be, since I have no husband?" Only now does Gabriel underscore the extraordinary type of motherhood to which Mary is being called:

"The Holy Spirit will come upon you, and the power of the Most High will overshadow you; therefore the child to be born will be called holy, the Son of God."

How will Mary, who is betrothed and still a virgin, bear a child? By the spirit and power of God, Gabriel says. Here we have the first clear indication of the virginal conception of the Messiah.

Furthermore, we see that Jesus' filial relationship with God far surpasses that of any king in David's dynasty. Jesus will be called Son of God not simply because of his *role* as Davidic heir and Messiah but because of his unique divine origin. Gabriel tells Mary that she will conceive through God's extraordinary intervention of sending the Holy Spirit upon her, and *this* is the reason for calling him God's Son: "*Therefore* the child to be born will be called holy, the Son of God."

God and Man

Early Christians saw Mary's conceiving Jesus by the power of the Holy Spirit as an important sign of Christ's humanity and divinity. On one hand, it points to his divine nature by highlighting his unique divine origin. By the power of God's Spirit, Mary really becomes the mother of her God. As the *Catechism of the Catholic Church* explains:

> The One whom she conceived as man by the Holy Spirit, who truly became her Son according to the flesh, was none other than the Father's eternal Son, the second person of the Holy Trinity. Hence the Church confesses that Mary is truly "Mother of God" (*Theotokos*). (#495)

On the other hand, the church fathers also saw the virginal conception as a sign that the divine Son of God really became human, taking the flesh of his mother Mary. Within the first century of Christianity, Saint Ignatius of Antioch, for example, emphasized that the Son of God really entered into the human family and really took on human flesh that he received in the virgin's womb. God did not just *appear* as a man, but he truly became one of us in Jesus, experiencing birth, life, suffering and even death. Ignatius once told his followers:

> You are firmly convinced about our Lord, who is truly of the race of David according to the flesh, Son of God according to the will and power of God, truly born of a virgin…he was truly nailed to a tree for us in his flesh under Pontius Pilate…he truly suffered, as he is also truly risen.[4]

Mary's *Fiat*

Let us now step back and consider all that has happened to Mary in this brief encounter with Gabriel.

First, an angel visits the young woman from the small town of Nazareth. This alone would have been quite startling. Second, in hearing the angel's words "The Lord is with you" and "You have found favor with God," Mary probably realizes that God is calling her to some daunting task. She is to play a pivotal role in God's plan of salvation, as did Noah, Abraham, Moses, David and many other key figures in Israel's history who have gone before her.

Third, she finds out that she will be expecting a baby. Fourth, she is informed that this child just happens to be the long-awaited Messiah who will restore Israel's kingdom and bring the history of the world to its climactic moment. Fifth, she will conceive of this child not through natural means but through a miraculous conception brought about by God's Holy Spirit.

Finally—as if all this were not already astonishing enough—the angel tells her that this child is the divine Son of God.

That's a lot to swallow in one short conversation with an angel! All of this was given to Mary in a conversation that could have taken place in about a minute or two.

It is difficult to imagine what Mary was going through in those brief moments. Some people would have requested a little time to think about and process all that was just said. Others might have responded, "Why me?" Still others might have just fainted! While we don't know much about Mary's emotions and thoughts at the angel's annunciation, the one response Luke does record for us is one of complete trust: "And Mary said, 'Behold, I am the handmaid of the Lord; *let it be to me according to your word*'" (Luke 1:38, emphasis added).

What is interesting about Mary's response is that the Greek word in this verse for "let it be to me" expresses not a passive acceptance but a joyful wishing or desiring on Mary's part.[5] Mary does not passively agree to go along with this challenging vocation, but upon hearing of her extraordinary maternal mission, she positively desires it and fully embraces God's call for her to serve as the mother of the Messiah.

A Model Disciple

This is why many scholars—Catholic and Protestant alike—recognize Mary as the first Christian disciple and a model follower of Jesus.[6] In Luke's Gospel Jesus says that those who hear the word of God and keep it are blessed and are included in his family of disciples (see Luke 8:21). Mary fits this description better than anyone else in Luke's Gospel. From the very beginning she accepts God's word from the angel Gabriel and calls herself the servant of the

Lord. In subsequent scenes we will see that Mary responds promptly to her relative Elizabeth's needs as soon as she learns from Gabriel that Elizabeth is pregnant in her old age.

Furthermore, she is counted among the "blessed" disciples in Luke's Gospel. Not only will Elizabeth call Mary *blessed* for believing God's word (1:45), but Mary herself will say that *all generations* will call her *blessed* (1:48). Similarly, like a good disciple who hears God's word and keeps it, Mary will "*keep* in her heart" the angel's joyous message at Jesus' birth (2:19) and Christ's words to her when she finds him in the temple (2:51).

Finally, Luke shows us Mary persevering in faithfulness throughout her life, devoting herself to prayer and to the life of the early Christian community in the days following her Son's resurrection and ascension into heaven (see Acts 1:14).

Throughout her life, therefore, Mary's acceptance of God's word is exemplary. As the first person to accept God's word in the new covenant, her obedience anticipates the response many will make to Christ's call to follow him in his public ministry and throughout the Christian era.

Her faith also serves as a model for how we as Christians should follow Christ in our own lives today. Like Mary, we should respond to God's word promptly, joyfully and with a servant's heart—not simply with a passive acceptance, but with an active embrace and hunger to do God's will. This is one reason why we consider Mary to be not only the first Christian disciple but the most perfect disciple of all time.

Reflection Questions

1. Read Luke 1:26-27. From these verses, name four things we know about Mary's life *before* Gabriel appeared to her.

What do these simple facts tell us about the future mother of the Messiah?

2. What does it mean that Mary was "betrothed" to Joseph? Were they married? Were they living together? Had they consummated their marriage?

3. What is the significance of Mary's marrying into the family of a man from "the house of David"? Did this credential carry a lot of weight in the first century? Explain.

4. Read Luke 1:28-29. Considering Gabriel's words "The Lord is with you," why might Mary be greatly troubled at *the kind of greeting* he gave her?

   ✳ How were these words used in the Old Testament (see Exodus 3:12; Joshua 1:9; Judges 6:12)?

   ✳ What would this greeting have told Mary about her vocation?

5. Now consider the liturgical prayer that the priest says to us at Mass: "The Lord be with you." In light of the biblical background for this prayer, what might this prayer tell us about *our own* mission as Christians?

6. Read 2 Samuel 7:9, 12-16. What does God promise to do for David and his descendants?

7. Now read Luke 1:31-35. What themes from 2 Samuel 7 does the angel draw on in his description of the child Mary will have? What does this tell us about the child?

8. Read Luke 1:38.

    Pope John Paul II has explained that Mary's response to the angel in this verse is not a passive submission to God's will. The words imply an active acceptance and a joyful desiring to serve God in this way. We can learn a lot from Mary's response. Sometimes we may do the right thing but only begrudgingly. ("I *have* to go to church today." "I guess I *have* to be nice to this difficult person"). Instead of looking at the sacrifice involved, Mary joyfully embraces God's will for her and enthusiastically pursues it. Describe one area in your life where you can imitate Mary's response by more joyfully doing God's will.

9. Read Luke 8:19-21 and 11:27-28. According to these verses, who is part of Christ's family? Who is blessed?

10. At first glance, the two passages above may give the impression that Jesus is distancing himself from his mother by giving priority to his spiritual family of disciples over his physical family members. However, Luke's Gospel actually portrays his natural mother, Mary, as a preeminent member of Christ's spiritual family of disciples. How is Mary presented as a model follower of Christ in the following verses?

    * Luke 1:38

    * Luke1:42-45

    * Luke 1:48

    * Luke 2:19

✸   Luke 2:51

✸   See also John 19:25-27 and Acts 1:14

What insights do you have from these verses about how you can
learn from Mary's example?

CHAPTER THREE

Blessed Among Women
The Visitation
(Luke 1:39-56)

IN THE OPENING CHAPTERS of Luke's Gospel, John the Baptist and Jesus seem to be living parallel lives; what happens to one happens to the other.

Consider the following parallels: Before John and Jesus are even born, their parents receive knowledge of their conceptions in an almost identical manner. The angel *Gabriel* visits both Zechariah (John's father) and Mary (Jesus' mother) (1:19, 26). Both parents respond in fear, being *troubled* by their angelic guest (1:12, 29), and both are assured by Gabriel, *"Do not be afraid"* (1:13, 30). Gabriel tells both that they will have a *son* born miraculously to them (1:13, 35) and that these sons will play a crucial role in God's saving plan (1:15-17, 32-33, 35). Gabriel instructs both parents what to name their sons (1:13, 31) and foretells that both children will be *great* (1:15, 32). Both Zechariah and Mary respond with *questions* for the angel, "How shall I know this?" and "How can this be...?" (1:18, 34).

Luke's Gospel goes on to demonstrate the parallels between John and Jesus in their early years, following a fourfold pattern. In narrating the beginning of John the Baptist's life, Luke tells us first about John's *birth* (1:57), second about his *circumcision and naming* (1:58-66), third about his father's *response of praising God* in thanksgiving for the child (1:67-79), and fourth about *the maturing of John,* who "grew and became strong in the spirit" (1:80).[1]

After these opening scenes about John, Luke proceeds to tell the story of Jesus' childhood, following the same fourfold scheme: he narrates Christ's *birth* (2:1-20), his *circumcision and naming* (2:21), Simeon's *response of praising God* in thanksgiving for this child (2:29-32), and the *maturing of Jesus,* who "grew and became strong, filled with wisdom" (2:40).

John's Birth Announcement	Jesus' Birth Announcement
The angel Gabriel appears to Zechariah (1:19).	The angel Gabriel appears to Mary (1:26).
Zechariah responds with fear, being "troubled" (1:12).	Mary responds with fear, being "troubled" (1:29).
"Do not be afraid" (1:13).	"Do not be afraid" (1:30).
Gabriel announces a miraculous birth (1:13).	Gabriel announces a miraculous birth (1:31).
"Elizabeth will bear you a son, and you shall call his name John" (1:13).	"You will...bear a son, and you shall call his name Jesus" (1:31).
"He will be great before the Lord" (1:15).	"He will be great" (1:32).
"How shall I know this? For I am an old man and my wife is advanced in years" (1:18).	"How shall this be, since I have no husband?" (1:34).

John's Birth	Jesus' Birth
Birth of John (1:57)	Birth of Jesus (2:1-20).
Circumcision and naming of John (1:58-66).	Circumcision and naming of Jesus (2:21).
Zechariah praises God in thanksgiving for the child John (1:67-79).	Simeon praises God in thanksgiving for the child Jesus (2:29-32).
"And the child grew and became strong in the spirit" (1:80).	"And the child grew and became strong, filled with wisdom" (2:40).

Déjà Vu?

By the time we finish Luke's infancy narrative as a whole, the story of Jesus' birth following on the heels of the accounts about John's might appear like *déjà vu* to the reader. Far from being coincidental, however, these extensive parallels in the narrative suggest Luke's deliberate attempt to encourage us to view the story of John and the story of Jesus together. In the end we will see that the two accounts are really part of the same story: the drama of God's intervening in the lives of these two families to bring about his plan of salvation through the miraculously God-given children they will raise.

We see this most clearly in our present scene, commonly known as "the visitation." When Mary travels to visit Elizabeth, the two families come together, and both expectant mothers appear on the same stage, sharing their joy about the amazing events taking place in their lives.

Seasoned Greetings

> In those days Mary arose and went with haste into the hill country, to a city of Judah, and she entered the house of Zechariah and greeted Elizabeth.
>
> —LUKE 1:39-40

What Mary sets out to do in this scene is remarkable. She just learned from the angel Gabriel that her relative Elizabeth is expecting a child in her old age. Mary also just found out that she is expecting a child of her own (1:30-37). However, this does not keep her from going to help Elizabeth in her time of need. Even though her own pregnancy is just getting underway, Mary leaves Nazareth "with haste" and travels about seventy miles south to the hill country around Jerusalem in order to serve her kinswoman. The young Virgin of Nazareth comes to assist Elizabeth during her last trimester with John, while her own first trimester with Jesus is just beginning.

Luke tells us that when Mary arrives at Elizabeth's home, *she greets her*. Such a salutation seems to fit ancient Jewish customs, which would call for Mary, the younger, to greet Elizabeth, her elder, first. Furthermore, Elizabeth's coming from an honorable priestly family would add even more to the expectation that Mary would show respect in addressing her kinswoman first.[2]

The rather surprising part of this encounter, however, is not in Mary's greeting Elizabeth but in the way Elizabeth in turn greets Mary:

> And when Elizabeth heard the greeting of Mary, the babe leaped in her womb; and Elizabeth was filled with the Holy Spirit and she exclaimed with a loud cry, "Blessed are you among women, and blessed is the fruit of your womb! And why is this granted me, that the mother of my Lord should

come to me? For behold, when the voice of your greeting came
to my ears, the babe in my womb leaped for joy. And blessed is
she who believed that there would be a fulfillment of what was
spoken to her from the Lord."

—LUKE 1:41-45

Elizabeth's words bring to mind the way someone in Judea would
greet and praise a superior for his or her higher status and for being
blessed by God.[3] Such honor given to a younger relative, however,
would be quite unusual. Why all these accolades for Mary?

Filled with the Holy Spirit, Elizabeth has prophetic insight
into the uniqueness of Mary's motherhood. Not only does she
realize that Mary is pregnant, but she understands that Mary has
become the mother of Israel's Messiah. In awe over the mystery
taking place in Mary's womb, Elizabeth, in extraordinary fashion,
honors her younger kinswoman and acknowledges her as "the
mother of my Lord" and "blessed…among women."

Royal Treatment

Let us consider what these titles would have meant in ancient
Judaism. First, by calling Mary "the mother of my Lord,"
Elizabeth hails her as the mother of the King. In the Old
Testament "my Lord" was a court expression given to honor the
anointed king (see, for example, 2 Samuel 24:21; Psalm 110:1).
Thus, when Elizabeth addresses Mary as "the mother of my
Lord," she is recognizing her as the royal mother of Israel's
Messiah.

And this is no small honor, for as the mother of the King,
Mary would be seen as the queen in her son's kingdom. In the
ancient Jewish world, the queenship in the Davidic kingdom was
given not to the king's wife but to the king's mother. Kings in the

Old Testament often had large harems; King Solomon, for example, had seven hundred wives (see 1 Kings 11:3). One couldn't bestow the queenship on seven hundred women! However, each king had only one mother, so the queenship was given to her.

Therefore, when Elizabeth addresses Mary as "the mother of my Lord," she is saying a lot. From an ancient Jewish biblical perspective, Mary, as the mother of the Messiah-King, would be understood to be the queen-mother in her son's kingdom.[4]

Blessed Among Women

Second, the description "blessed among women" would bring to mind the Old Testament heroines Jael and Judith. After Jael defeated a pagan general who was oppressing God's people, the prophetess Deborah proclaimed, "Most blessed of women be Jael" (Judges 5:24). Similarly, when Judith defeated a pagan commander who was attempting to overtake a Jewish town, Uzziah said to her: "O daughter, you are blessed by the Most High God above all women on earth" (Judith 13:18). Jael and Judith were blessed specifically because the Lord used them to rescue his people from the attacks of their enemies.

Standing in this tradition, Mary is called "blessed among women" because she too will be instrumental in God's plan for saving Israel. However, Mary's role has one crucial difference from those of these warrior women of old. Mary won't be engaging in a physical battle. Rather, she will participate in God's saving plan through the son she is carrying in her womb.

Elizabeth tells Mary that she is "blessed among women" because "blessed is the fruit of your womb." Mary is blessed because she will bear Israel's Messiah, and he will be the one to accomplish God's ultimate plan of salvation. And as Luke's narrative will gradually explain, this Messiah will save Israel not simply from their political or military enemies but from the real evil every human person faces: sin.

Leaping for Joy

Even the prenatal John the Baptist recognizes the uniqueness of Mary's presence among them, as he is filled with the Holy Spirit and leaps in his mother's womb when Mary arrives (1:41). Recall how Gabriel foretold that John would be filled with the Holy Spirit and have a prophetic mission "even from his mother's womb" (1:15). Gabriel's prediction comes true in this scene, as John's mother is filled with the Holy Spirit and John himself leaps in Elizabeth's womb in the presence of the Messiah, whom Mary bears. This act thus inaugurates John's ministry as the prophet who will herald the coming of the Messiah. It anticipates John's mission in his adult life to prepare the way for Christ.

Here we begin to see that, while the parallels between John and Jesus show a close relationship between these providential sons, it is not a relationship of equals. Luke's Gospel already has hinted at Jesus' superiority. Although both children are conceived miraculously, Mary's conceiving of Jesus by the Spirit and power of God as a virgin far surpasses the wonder of Elizabeth's conceiving John by natural means in her old age. Though both children are called great, John is said to be "great before the Lord" (1:15), while Jesus is called "great" in his own right without qualification (1:32). John is portrayed as the ultimate prophet to *prepare the way for* the Lord (1:15-18), while Jesus *is* the Messiah-King and Son of God whom John will be heralding (1:32-35).

Now in the Visitation scene, the priestly family shows deference to the kingly one: Elizabeth honors Mary as "the mother of my Lord" and "blessed among women," while John joyfully recognizes the presence of the Messiah by leaping in his mother's womb.

The Ark of the Covenant

Luke's narrative highlights Jesus' exalted status most profoundly by portraying his mother in ways that would recall the most sacred vessel in all of Israel: the ark of the covenant. The ark housed three objects of great importance: (1) a jar containing the *manna* (the heavenly bread that fell in the desert to feed the Israelites in the time of Moses); (2) the remains of the stone tablets upon which God had written the *Ten Commandments*; and (3) the *staff of Aaron*, the first high priest of Israel (Hebrews 9:4).

Most important, however, *the holy presence of God* hovered over the ark in the form of a cloud. That is why the ark resided in the most sacred chamber of the temple, called "the Holy of Holies." Indeed, one could say that it was God's presence over the ark of the covenant that made the Holy of Holies holy!

In a climactic moment from the life of David, the king brought the ark to Jerusalem. It will be helpful to recall some specific points from this pivotal story about the ark's journey to David's capital city in 2 Samuel 6. David arose and went up from Baale-judah (*the hill country of Judea*) to bring the ark of the covenant to Jerusalem (see 2 Samuel 6:2). On the way there, David, in awe of God's power in the ark, paused and said, "*How can the ark of the Lord come to me?*" (6:9). The ark remained in the *house of Obededom* for *three months*, blessing Obededom and all his household (6:10-11). Then the ark was brought up to Jerusalem in a grand procession, with the people rejoicing and *shouting* (6:15) and with king David himself *leaping* and dancing before it (6:16).

Luke's portrayal of Mary's journey to visit Elizabeth brings to mind in many ways the ark's journey to Jerusalem. Just like the ark, Mary travels to the *hill country of Judah* (Luke 1:39). As the ark resided in the house of Obededum *for three months,* Mary remains in the house of Zechariah (Luke 1:40) for the same amount of time (Luke 1:56). As the people in Jerusalem welcomed the ark with shouting and rejoicing, so Elizabeth "*exclaimed* with a loud cry" when she greeted Mary (Luke 1:42). And as David leaped and danced before the ark of the Lord, so does John the Baptist *leap* in Elizabeth's womb when Mary draws near (Luke 1:41).

Finally, both the ark and Mary provoke similar questions. Just as David asked on the ark's arrival, "How can the ark of the Lord come to me?" so Elizabeth welcomes Mary, "And why is this granted to me, that the mother of my Lord should come to me?" (Luke 1:43).[5]

Even before the Visitation scene, Luke's Gospel hints at parallels between Mary and the ark. In Luke 1:35 the angel Gabriel tells Mary that "the power of the Most High will *overshadow* you." The Greek verb Luke uses for "overshadow" is the same verb used in Exodus 40:35 to describe how God's presence and glory in the form of a cloud *overshadowed the sanctuary, which housed the ark of the covenant* at Mount Sinai. Just as God's holy presence hovered over the ark in the desert, his presence overshadows Mary at the Annunciation.[6]

Perhaps the most striking parallel between Mary and the ark of the covenant comes in Luke 1:42, which tells us that

Elizabeth "exclaimed" when she greeted Mary. That may seem like a small, insignificant detail, until we realize that the Greek verb for "exclaim" that Luke chose for this verse (*anaphonein*) is used everywhere else in the Bible in relation to the ark of the covenant. In fact, in every other place where the word *anaphonein* appears, it depicts a specific kind of exclaiming: that of the Levitical priests shouting out in song and praising God *before the ark of the covenant.*[7]

Thus Elizabeth exclaims before Mary as the priests exclaimed before the ark. Like the priests who sang praises to God, who dwelt over the ark of the covenant, Elizabeth—who herself is from an honorable priestly family—shouts praises (*anaphonein*) before her Lord residing in Mary's womb.

Indeed, Mary is like a new ark of the covenant, bearing the presence of God in her womb. And just as the ark carried the manna, so Mary carries in her womb the child who will be known as the true bread of life (see John 6:48-51). Just as the ark contained the Ten Commandments, so Mary bears the one who is the fulfillment of the Law (see Matthew 5:17). And just as the ark carried the staff of the high priest Aaron, so does Mary carry in her womb the true high priest who will offer his life on the cross for our sins (see Hebrews 8:1-7).

The Magnificat

Now we turn to a high point in Luke's Gospel so far: Mary's hymn-like response to Elizabeth's greeting in verses 46-55. Commonly called the Magnificat (taken from the first words, "My soul *magnifies* the Lord"), these verses represent the first of four canticles that appear in Luke's account of Christ's birth. One scholar has described these canticles as "pauses" in the narrative.

They bring the rush of action to a halt and give the reader a chance to reflect on the *meaning* of these events surrounding the birth of the Messiah.[8]

Before we look at the Magnificat itself, consider all that has happened so far in the first chapter of Luke's Gospel. In the opening scene we discover that Zechariah the priest has just been chosen by lot for the once-in-a-lifetime opportunity to offer incense in the temple. As we accompany Zechariah into the inner chambers of the sanctuary, we see him suddenly confronted by an angel of the Lord. And the angel announces an astonishing message: Zechariah's aging and barren wife will miraculously bear a son. Even more remarkable is that this son will be Israel's long-awaited prophet, the new Elijah, who will prepare the way for the Messiah.

In the second scene the reader finds the same angel appearing to Mary in Galilee, but this time he announces an even more remarkable miracle: Mary will conceive a child as a virgin by the power of the Holy Spirit. And this child not only will be the Messiah-King who will bring all of Israel's prophecies and hopes to fulfillment; he will be the Son of God himself. With little reflection in the narrative on this most profound mystery, we are then whisked away into the next scene, set seventy miles to the south in Judea, where Mary travels "with haste" to visit her kinswoman Elizabeth.

There certainly is a lot for readers to digest in these three opening scenes of Luke's Gospel! We feel the need to take a moment to process all the dramatic events that have been rapidly unfolding before us at the dawn of Christianity. Mary's song gives readers just that opportunity, serving as a contemplative moment—a pause in the narrative flow. In the Magnificat the reader is invited to join Mary in reflecting on the meaning of these events and praising God for all that he is already accomplishing in her life—and is about to accomplish for the rest of the world.

Play It Again, Samuel!

And Mary said,
"My soul magnifies the Lord,
and my spirit rejoices in God my Savior,
for he has regarded the low estate of his handmaiden.[9]
For behold, henceforth all generations will call me blessed;
for he who is mighty has done great things for me,
and holy is his name.
And his mercy is on those who fear him
from generation to generation.
He has shown strength with his arm,
he has scattered the proud in the imagination of their hearts,
he has put down the mighty from their thrones,
and exalted those of low degree; [10]
he has filled the hungry with good things,
and the rich he has sent empty away.
He has helped his servant Israel,
in remembrance of his mercy,
as he spoke to our fathers,
to Abraham and to his posterity forever."
And Mary remained with her about three months, and
returned to her home.

—LUKE 1:46-56

If we were living in first-century Judea, many of the words from Mary's song would sound very familiar to our ears. It would seem somewhat like a remake of "an oldie" from the Jewish tradition— Hannah's song in 1 Samuel 2:1-10.

Hannah was an Israelite woman who was ridiculed for being barren. She cried out to the Lord for a child, and God

48

eventually intervened in her life, blessing her with a son, Samuel, who was called to renew the people of Israel. Hannah dedicated her son in the temple to the Lord's service, and she sang a famous canticle of praise, thanking God for comforting her in her affliction and giving her a child.

> My heart exults in the Lord;
> my strength is exalted in the Lord.
> My mouth derides my enemies,
> because I rejoice in thy salvation.
>
> There is none holy like the Lord,
> there is none besides thee;
> there is no rock like our God.
> Talk no more so very proudly,
> let not arrogance come from your mouth;
> for the Lord is a God of knowledge,
> and by him actions are weighed.
> The bows of the mighty are broken,
> but the feeble gird on strength.
> Those who were full have hired themselves out for bread,
> but those who were hungry have ceased to hunger.
> The barren has borne seven,
> but she who has many children is forlorn.
> The Lord kills and brings to life;
> he brings down to Sheol and raises up.
> The Lord makes poor and makes rich;
> he brings low, he also exalts.
> He raises up the poor from the dust;
> he lifts the needy from the ash heap,
> to make them sit with princes
> and inherit a seat of honor.
> For the pillars of the earth are the Lord's,
> and on them he has set the world.

> He will guard the feet of his faithful ones;
> but the wicked shall be cut off in darkness;
> for not by might shall a man prevail.
> The adversaries of the LORD shall be broken to pieces;
> against them he will thunder in heaven.
> The LORD will judge the ends of the earth;
> he will give strength to his king,
> and exalt the power of his anointed.
>
> —1 SAMUEL 2:1-10

Here we can see that Mary's song echoes numerous themes and images from the song of Hannah. Both songs praise the Lord as savior and acknowledge him as holy. Both songs announce how the mighty and rich will be cast down, while the lowly and the poor will be raised up. Those who have their fill will come away empty, while the hungry will hunger no more. These parallels demonstrate that Mary views herself as standing in the tradition of women like Hannah whom God has raised up from their afflictions.

Like Hannah, Mary has conceived a child through the miraculous intervention of God in her life. Like Hannah, Mary will dedicate her son in the temple (see Luke 2:22-24). Like Hannah, Mary responds with a song of praise and thanksgiving for the providential child she is given. Finally, while Hannah's song culminates with the announcement of the future coming of a king, Mary's song rejoices in the fact that God has given to Israel the long-awaited Messiah-King whom she now carries in her womb.

Hannah's Song (1 Samuel 2:1-10)	**Mary's Song (Luke 1:46-55)**
My heart exults in the LORD; my strength is exalted in the LORD. My mouth derides my enemies, because I rejoice in thy salvation (2:1).	My soul magnifies the LORD, and my spirit rejoices in God my Savior (1:46).
There is none holy like the LORD (2:2)	Holy is his name (1:49).
The bows of the mighty are broken, but the feeble gird on strength. Those who were full have hired themselves out for bread, but those who were hungry have ceased to hunger.… The LORD makes poor and makes rich; he brings low, he also exalts. He raises up the poor from the dust; he lifts the needy from the ash heap, to make them sit with princes and inherit a seat of honor (2:4-5, 7-8).	He has shown strength with his arm, he has scattered the proud in the imagination of their hearts. He has put down the mighty from their thrones, and exalted those of low degree; he has filled the hungry with good things, and the rich he has sent empty away (1:51-53).

Upward Mobility

A second point standing out from Mary's song is the theme of reversal in both the first and the second halves of the canticle. In the first half Mary describes how God has looked upon her own lowliness and done great things for her (1:46-50), while in the second half she announces how God has looked mercifully upon all those of low estate and has raised them up from their afflictions (1:51-55). This movement from lowliness to exalta-tion—both in the individual Mary and in the people of God as a whole—is the key to understanding the Magnificat.

Let us begin by considering the first half of the canticle, where the camera lens is focused on Mary. The particular word Mary uses to describe her own "low estate" (*tapeinosin*) in 1:48 describes not simply a spiritual humility but a condition of great suffering. In fact, the word was commonly used in the Old Testament to depict the affliction of God's people when they were persecuted and oppressed but about to be rescued by God's saving hand (see Deuteronomy 26:7; 1 Samuel 9:16; 2 Kings 14:26). For example, recalling how God once freed Israel from its slavery in Egypt, Psalm 136 says: "It is he who remembered us in our *low estate*…and *rescued* us from our foes" (23-24, emphasis added).

With this background in mind, we can see that when Mary speaks of God's regard for her own "low estate" (*tapeinosin*), she views herself as in some sense being lifted up by God in the midst of her own suffering. Yet we are left wondering, "What is the nature of Mary's affliction?"

Considered within the social context of Roman and Herodian rule in first-century Galilee, Mary's "low estate" would bring to mind the pains experienced by many Jews who were suf-fering under foreign domination at that time. As one New Testament scholar has explained, "It is not that Mary has some personal and individual affliction; her affliction is simply that of God's people awaiting his saving intervention on their behalf."[11] Mary recognizes that God has looked upon her lowliness with mercy (1:50) and has "done great things" for her (1:49). He has taken this young Jewish virgin living under foreign domination in the insignificant town of Nazareth and has made her the mother of Israel's Messiah-King.

This prepares the way for understanding the second half of Mary's song, where the camera lens is pulled back so that we can see God's people as a whole—the people who have Mary as their premier member. Mary announces that what God has done for her he is about to do for all those of "low degree" (*tapeinous*) in Israel (1:52). God has remembered his covenant with Abraham and has come to help his people Israel (1:54-55). In the process, "the proud," "the mighty" and "the rich" will be cast down, while "those of low estate" (*tapeinous*) will be exalted, and "the hungry" will be filled.

The Rich and the Poor

To understand more fully what Mary is saying in this part of the Magnificat, it is important to note that in Luke's Gospel the words *rich* and *poor* are not simply economic terms. "The poor" refers not only to people in material poverty but, more broadly, to all the marginalized and downtrodden in society. Throughout Luke's Gospel, in fact, "the poor" refers to a wide range of people, including the blind, the lame, the deaf and the lepers, as well as those burdened by socio-political injustices such as "the oppressed," "the captives," "the persecuted" and "the hungry."[12] In a similar manner, "the rich" is not simply a synonym for the economic upper class but a social term describing those who exploit, overlook or marginalize the various "poor" outcasts of society.

In light of this background, Mary is announcing a series of ironic reversals in society. God in his mercy has remembered the suffering and oppressed in Israel and will gather them into the kingdom of his Son, while "the proud," "the mighty" and "the rich," who oppose God's people, are about to be cast down.

As such, the connection between the two halves of Mary's song becomes clear: the way God exalts Mary in her lowliness (first half) anticipates how God will mercifully look upon the afflictions of *all* the lowly in Israel (second half). In other words, what God has done for Mary he is going to do for the rest of his people. Mary's song thus proclaims not just good news for Mary but good news for all of Israel.

The Song of the Church

Now we can see how Mary's song anticipates the major components of her Son's mission. As the subsequent chapters of Luke's Gospel will show, Jesus' public ministry embodies these dramatic reversals proclaimed by the Magnificat, whether it be in his healing the sick, feeding the hungry, extending fellowship to the estranged and forgiving sinners or in his confronting the social, political and religious leaders of the day. In fact, right at the heart of his teachings about the kingdom, we find Jesus proclaiming the same news of salvation announced in Mary's song. In the Beatitudes Jesus, like his mother in the Magnificat, announces blessing upon the poor, the hungry, the persecuted and the excluded, while he announces woe to the rich—those who are comfortable, socially accepted and having their fill (see Luke 6:20-26). Mary's Magnificat finds fulfillment in Christ's public ministry.

Mary's song also anticipates the prayer of the Church, which ceaselessly "proclaims the greatness of the Lord." In the first half of the Magnificat we join Mary in praising God for looking mercifully on her lowliness and inviting her to serve as the mother of Israel's Messiah. In the second half we contemplate the connection between Mary and our own lives in the Church today. What God has done for this lowly woman of Galilee he will do for all of us through her Son. He will meet us in our own lowliness and sufferings and do "great things" for us. Like a representative of all the faithful, Mary stands at the gateway of the new covenant as the first Christian disciple to receive the amazing mercy of God in Jesus.

Reflection Questions

1. Read Luke 1:39-40. Recall that Mary just became pregnant herself and has many of her own things to worry about now. Nevertheless, she embarks on a seventy-mile journey to visit her kinswoman Elizabeth.

   * What do these verses tell us about Mary's attentiveness to others' needs?

   * What happens when you become overwhelmed by your own preoccupations—stress at work, financial difficulties, family tensions, health problems and so on? Are you able to be as attentive to the needs of those around you?

   * What are some ways you can imitate Mary's example of prompt, joyful service to others in the midst of being weighed down by your own concerns?

2. Read Luke 1:41-45. What is extraordinary about the way Elizabeth greets Mary? How can you show additional respect toward those whom God has chosen to serve him in special ways?

3. "Ark of the Covenant" is a traditional title for Mary.

   ✳ How does Mary resemble the Old Testament ark of the covenant?

   ✳ Explain some ways in which Luke's Gospel portrays Mary as the new ark of the covenant. Name some of the parallels between what happens to the ark in 2 Samuel 6:2, 9-16 with what happens to Mary in Luke 1:39-45, 56.

   ✳ What does this tell us about Mary?

   ✳ How can you honor Mary as the bearer of God's Son to the world?

4. Read Luke 1:46-49 (the Magnificat). According to verses 48-49, what has God done for Mary?

5. Read Luke 1:50-55. In the second part of this song, Mary praises God for blessing all the faithful and suffering in Israel. What has God done for them?

6. Comparing the two parts of this song, what is the relationship between Mary and the rest of Israel?

7. How does Mary's song anticipate themes from Christ's public ministry (see Luke 6:20-26)? Describe a situation in which you have seen God's "reversal action" in your life?

CHAPTER FOUR

The Last Prophet
The Birth of John the Baptist
(Luke 1:57-80)

Now the time came for Elizabeth to be delivered, and she gave birth to a son. And her neighbors and kinsfolk heard that the Lord had shown great mercy to her, and they rejoiced with her. And on the eighth day they came to circumcise the child; and they would have named him Zechariah after his father, but his mother said, "Not so, he shall be called John." And they said to her, "None of your kindred is called by this name." And they made signs to his father, inquiring what he would have him called. And he asked for a writing tablet, and wrote, "His name is John." And they all marveled. And immediately his mouth was opened and his tongue loosed, and he spoke, blessing God. And fear came on all their neighbors. And all these things were talked about through all the hill country of Judea; and all who heard them laid them up in their hearts, saying, "What then will this child be?" For the hand of the Lord was with him.

—LUKE 1:57-66

ZECHARIAH FINALLY GETS A second chance. Nine months ago he doubted the angel's message to him in the temple. He simply could not believe that his barren wife would conceive and bear a child in her old age. Muted, Zechariah has had nine months to ponder Gabriel's message over and over in his mind and humbly reconsider his own disbelief. Now he has witnessed Gabriel's words come to fulfillment through his wife's pregnancy.

The opportunity for a second chance arises on the eighth day of the child's life, when it is time to circumcise and name him. As witnesses to this covenant ritual, Elizabeth's relatives and friends play a role in naming the child, and they want to name him after the father (1:59). Elizabeth, on the other hand, favors calling the child John (1:60).

What is interesting for us as readers is that we know John is the name Gabriel instructed Zechariah to give to the child (see 1:13), yet Elizabeth seems to arrive at the same conclusion on her own—independent of any angelic revelation or conversation with her husband, who has been mute for the last nine months.

This choice, however, is incredibly frustrating for the neighbors and kinsfolk. They cannot understand why Elizabeth would break from the Jewish custom of passing on family names. They protest, "None of your kindred is called by this name." Hoping Zechariah will overturn Elizabeth's decision, they motion to him (indicating he is deaf as well as mute), and they give him a writing tablet so that he can inscribe his choice for the child's name. To the great surprise of the village, the muted father confirms Elizabeth's choice by writing, "His name is John."

What's in a Name?

This is a crucial moment for Zechariah because it is the first time we see him cooperating with the Lord's plan as revealed by Gabriel. In the temple Zechariah responded to the angel's message with doubt. Now, after nine quiet months to consider the angel's words and witness their fulfillment, Zechariah has come to greater faith. He obeys the angel's command and names the child John. As soon as he does this, his punishment comes to an end. His mouth is "immediately" opened, and he can speak again.

Understandably, the neighbors and relatives are astonished at the events that have just taken place. Consider all that they have witnessed this day: First, they were surprised by Elizabeth's desire to name the child John. Then they marveled when the deaf and mute Zechariah picked the same unexpected name as Elizabeth. Now they are left stunned when at the moment Zechariah declares his son's name to be John, he is suddenly able to speak again.

Those present sense God's hand in these events. In awe, they recognize that they are caught up in something much larger than the circumcision and naming of this child. God must have some special purpose for the newborn. Fear of the Lord comes upon them, and they wonder, "What then will this child be?"

The Benedictus

Zechariah uses his newfound speech to thank God in a hymn-like praise that has come to be known as the Benedictus (the Latin translation of the first word of his praise, "Blessed"). This is the second canticle in Luke's Gospel, and like Mary's Magnificat, the Benedictus serves as a pause in the narrative, giving the reader a chance to reflect on the saving events that are taking place.

Proclaiming his son's role as the herald of the Messiah, Zechariah is inspired by the Holy Spirit and speaks as a prophet. And he offers this song as a prophetic answer to his friends' question, "What then will this child be?"

Let us consider the first half of this song:

> And his father Zechariah was filled with the Holy Spirit, and
>   prophesied, saying,
> "Blessed be the Lord God of Israel,
> for he has visited and redeemed his people,
> and has raised up a horn of salvation for us
> in the house of his servant David,
> as he spoke by the mouth of his holy prophets from of old,
> that we should be saved from our enemies,
> and from the hand of all who hate us;
> to perform the mercy promised to our fathers,
> and to remember his holy covenant,
> the oath which he swore to our father Abraham, to grant us
> that we, being delivered from the hand of our enemies,
> might serve him without fear,
> in holiness and righteousness before him all the days of
>   our life.
>
> —LUKE 1:67-75

The language Zechariah uses in this hymn of praise would have stirred up much hope in the hearts of his neighbors and relatives listening that day. If we were there, we would hear in Zechariah's song an announcement that the history of the world has reached a decisive turning point and that God is about to act in our lives in a most dramatic fashion.

The first thing that might grab people's attention is Zechariah's proclamation that God has "visited" his people. This language is not about God's stopping by to say hello. Rather, the depiction of God "visiting" his people served as a powerful image in the Old Testament to describe how the Lord mercifully looked upon his people's sufferings and freed them from their afflictions (see Genesis 21:1; Exodus 4:31; Ruth 1:6; Psalm 80:14; 106:4).

For example, when God "visited" the Israelites during their slavery in Egypt, he looked upon their hardships and then sent Moses to deliver them from their foes (see Exodus 4:31). Now in the Benedictus, Zechariah is announcing similar astonishing news. God has "visited" his people again. In other words, the same saving hand that rescued Israel from the Egyptians is about to save the nation from its current hardships under Roman rule.

A New Exodus

A second amazing point from Zechariah's canticle is his saying that God has "redeemed" his people. The term *redeem* originally was used to describe the Jewish custom of buying back something that once was one's own but had fallen into the hands of another. The word in fact means "to buy back."

The Old Testament came to use redemption imagery spiritually to depict God's activity of freeing his people from their enemies. In fact, the redemption story *par excellence* was the Exodus, when Yahweh "bought back" the Israelites from slavery, releasing them from their oppression in Egypt.

What is most significant about the word *redemption* is that prophets like Isaiah spoke of Yahweh's performing another great act of redemption for his people in the future. The prophets foretold that one day God would *redeem* the Jews from their current enemies as he freed their ancestors from Pharaoh in the first Exodus (see, for example, Isaiah 43:1; 44:22-23; 52:9). After hundreds of years of foreign domination, Jews in the time of Zechariah would be longing for this new exodus to arrive. They would be yearning for God to fulfill the prophecies and "buy them back" from their oppression. Therefore, when Zechariah speaks of God's *redeeming* his people, he is proclaiming that the long-awaited new exodus is finally here!

A Horn of Salvation

Zechariah's song reaches a climactic point when he says, "God...has raised up a *horn* of salvation for us *in the house of his servant David.*" These words would have signaled that God is now sending the much anticipated Messiah to restore the kingdom to Israel.

In the ancient Near East the horn was a symbol of strength. However, when Zechariah speaks of a horn rising "*in the house of his servant David,*" he has a very specific power in mind—the strength of a new King coming from the Davidic dynasty. In fact, Zechariah's words echo the royal hymn of Psalm 132, which celebrated God's covenant with King David and his descendants. There the Lord said, "I will make a horn to sprout for David; I have prepared a lamp for my anointed" (Psalm 132:17).

Although the Davidic dynasty has remained dormant for hundreds of years under foreign occupation, the prophets foretold that God one day would send a new son of David to restore the shattered kingdom. That new anointed king became known as the "Messiah" (meaning, "anointed one"). It is this Messiah-King whom Zechariah is announcing in this song. By using the Davidic "horn" imagery, Zechariah proclaims that a new era is dawning over Israel: The long-awaited Messiah is now rising, and the restoration of the great Davidic dynasty is on the horizon. This kingdom will bring Israel salvation.

The Real Enemy

What kind of salvation will this Messiah bring? The emphasis in the first half of Zechariah's song appears to be on a military or political liberation. After all, Zechariah portrays this salvation in terms of the Israelites being "saved from our enemies, and from the hand of all who hate us" (1:71). Similarly, he says Israel will be "delivered from our enemies" (1:74). For many Jews in Zechariah's day, "our enemies" and "all who hate us" easily would be identified as Rome, Herod and all those in league with these first-century oppressors of the Jewish people. Many hoped that God would quickly send the Messiah to free them from these foreign adversaries.

However, in the second half of the Benedictus we see rather clearly that the new Davidic king will not be leading the people in a political revolution or military takeover. Instead, he comes to offer a much more profound type of liberation: *He will save us from our sins.*

> "And you, child, will be called the prophet of the Most High;
> for you will go before the Lord to prepare his ways,
> to give knowledge of salvation to his people
> in the forgiveness of their sins,
> through the tender mercy of our God,
> when the day shall dawn upon us from on high
> to give light to those who sit in darkness and the shadow of
> death,
> to guide our feet into the way of peace."
> And the child grew and became strong in spirit, and he was in
> the wilderness till the day of his manifestation to Israel.
> —LUKE 1:76-80

These verses represent Zechariah's first words to his eight-day-old son. He turns to address John saying, "You, child, will be called the prophet of the Most High; for you will go before the Lord to prepare his ways" (1:76). Here Zechariah finally proclaims in front of all his neighbors and family members what the angel Gabriel told him privately in the inner courts of the temple nine months ago: His son will be Israel's last and greatest prophet—the one who will prepare the way for the Lord.

Zechariah goes on to say that John's mission as the Messiah's forerunner is to give people "knowledge of salvation." However, Zechariah makes clear where this salvation will be found: not in political action or military maneuvering but "in the forgiveness of their sins."

True Freedom

This is the first time in Luke's Gospel that God's plan of salvation for Israel is explicitly linked with the forgiveness of sins. Up to this point we have read about the Messiah's restoring the kingdom of David (see 1:32-33) and God's showing mercy on Israel by exalting the lowly and casting down the powerful and the rich (1:46-55). Even in the first half of the Benedictus we have read about God's visiting, redeeming and saving his people (1:67-75). As we have seen, many in first-century Judaism might have understood these themes in terms of social and political revolution.

However, Zechariah's song makes clear that God's plan for saving his people involves much more than freeing them from foreign armies, heavy taxes and oppressive governments. More importantly, God wants to free his people from sin.

Zechariah's song reminds all of us that we should see the sufferings of the world not only on a political or social level but primarily on a spiritual one. Even in the ancient Jewish tradition, the leaders and prophets of Israel interpreted their own suffering under foreign domination as a symptom of a greater illness—a broken covenant relationship with Yahweh (see, for example, Deuteronomy 28:15-68; Daniel 9:1-19). That is why focusing only on social and political suffering is merely to look at the surface of things. Zechariah's words remind us that the root problem for all social injustices lies in the hearts of men and women, and it is the spiritual illness there that God wants to treat. This is the illness that keeps the human family from true solidarity and from full union with God.

In sum, Zechariah prophesies that his son's vocation will be to prepare the way for the Messiah's mission to save Israel. John will carry out this role not by starting a military draft of aspiring revolutionaries or a rebel boot camp out in the desert, but by proclaiming to the people true salvation, which is found "in the forgiveness of their sins." In fact, the next time Zechariah's son appears in Luke's Gospel, he will be grown up and already out in the wilderness preparing the way of the Lord. He will be "preaching a baptism of repentance for the forgiveness of sins" (Luke 3:3), just as his father foretells in the Benedictus.

Reflection Questions

1. Let us consider some of the highlights from the life of Elizabeth. Read Luke 1:7 alongside 1:13, 1:24-25 and 1:57-58.

    ✳ Luke 1:58 says God has shown "great mercy" to Elizabeth. In what ways has the Lord's mercy been revealed in her life?

✴ What does the story of Elizabeth tell us about the way God hears our prayers and responds to our needs?

✴ Does God's help always come in the way we would expect and on the schedule we would like to set?

✴ The *Catechism of the Catholic Church* (#2735-2737) discusses how we sometimes feel our prayers are not being heard. In this section, the *Catechism* quotes an early Church Father who said "Do not be troubled if you do not immediately receive from God what you ask him; for he desires to do something even greater for you, while you cling to him in faith" (#2737). What do you think this statement about prayer means? How does it offer us comfort?

✴ Describe an area of your own life or in your family's life where you are waiting for God to show his "great mercy." How might the story of Elizabeth give you encouragement?

2. Read Luke 1:57-66. Why are the neighbors and relatives of Elizabeth frustrated with her desire to name her child John?

3. Why do the crowds marvel when Zechariah writes, "His name is John"?

4. Think for a moment about second chances: In Luke 1:5-23 Zechariah failed to trust Gabriel's message and was punished with being mute for the nine months of his wife's miraculous pregnancy. Now, in Luke 1:57-80, God gives Zechariah a chance to make up for his initial lack of faith.

What does this tell us about God's mercy? Describe a situation in which God gave you a second chance to set things right after having done something you later regretted.

5. Zechariah is able to speak again, and filled with the Holy Spirit, he utters a prophecy. In Luke 1:67-75 he addresses God and praises him for raising up "a horn of salvation" from the house of David. According to Luke 1:71-73, what kind of salvation will the Jews receive? In other words, from what will they be saved?

6. Now read the second part of this prophecy in Luke 1:76-77. Whom does Zechariah address in these verses? What will this person do? How will he fulfill his mission (see Luke 3:1-18)?

7. What does Zechariah say in these verses that helps clarify the kind of salvation God will bring to Israel?

8. Zechariah foretells that John the Baptist will be a great prophet who will prepare the way of the Messiah (Luke 1:76). However, answering this important call from God will not bring John a life of comfort and security but rather will entail many sacrifices and even cost him his life (see Luke 3:19-20; Matthew 14:1-12). In what ways might God be calling you to serve him more? What sacrifices and hardships might this entail?

CHAPTER FIVE

The Messiah's Birth
The Nativity
(Luke 2:1-20)

W HO WOULD BEST FIT the following description?

He is the divine "Son of God" and is called "Lord" and "savior of the whole world." He brings "good tidings" and "peace on earth," and his birthday is celebrated as a feast around the world, commemorating the beginning of a new era.

Most Christians would say this sounds a lot like Jesus. However, in the first-century context of Luke's Gospel, these were the well-known titles and honors showered on Caesar Augustus, the Roman emperor from 27 B.C. to A.D. 14.

Augustus was famous for reuniting the empire and restoring peace in the land. After the assassination of Julius Caesar in 44 B.C., Rome was thrown into political upheaval as different factions vied for power. Augustus eventually emerged as the sole ruler of Rome, bringing an end to the wars that plagued the empire.

In the eyes of many, Augustus saved Rome from destruction. He was thus hailed as "savior of the whole world," for he ushered in a new age—the age of the *Pax Romana* (the Roman peace). He eventually was called "son of God" and worshiped as a deity. His date of birth even was celebrated in some parts of the empire as "the birthday of the god," for his coming was said to bring "good news" for the whole world.

Luke's Gospel tells a different story about the climax of the world's history. The birthday that inaugurated a new era for the world took place not in a palace in Rome but in a little dwelling in Bethlehem. And the real Savior didn't bring peace to the nations through Roman force and domination but by becoming a man, so that he might offer his life on the cross to free us from our sins.

Indeed, Luke subverts the imperial propaganda by showing how Jesus—not Caesar—is the true "Son of God" (see 1:35) and the real Lord and "Savior" of the world (2:11). Jesus is the one who brings true "peace" on earth (2:14) and whose day of birth brings "good news," marking the dawn of a new period in the history of humanity (2:10).

The City of David

> In those days a decree went out from Casear Augustus that all the world should be enrolled. This was the first enrollment, when Quirinius was governor of Syria. And all went to be enrolled, each to his own city. And Joseph also went up from Galilee, from the city of Nazareth, to Judea, to the city of David, which is called Bethlehem, because he was of the house and lineage of David, to be enrolled with Mary, his betrothed, who was with child. And while they were there, the time came for her to be delivered. And she gave birth to her first-born son and wrapped him in swaddling cloths, and laid him in a manger, because there was no place for them in the inn.
>
> —LUKE 2:1-7

Highlighting Christ's universal mission, Luke places the birth of Jesus on the worldwide stage of Caesar Augustus' call for a census throughout the empire. The purpose of such a census would be to regularize the collection of taxes. Luke draws our attention to this census, mentioning it four times in verses 1-6, thereby giving more information about the enrollment than about the actual birth of Jesus.

Why does Luke focus on the census? Being forced to submit to a Roman enrollment and to pay the required taxes would have been a difficult reminder for the Jews of their oppressed condition under Roman rule. For Luke's Gospel the census thus serves as a symbol of Rome's control over Israel and the rest of the world. In a single decree Augustus makes his presence felt by families throughout the empire who are uprooted and forced to travel to their ancestral towns to participate in the emperor's census.

One of those families on the move is Joseph's. Being from the house and lineage of David, Joseph must travel to Bethlehem, the city of his family's origins. He takes his pregnant wife with him to be enrolled in "the city of David."

On one level, the story of Mary and Joseph's traveling to Bethlehem highlights Caesar's worldwide dominance, which reaches all the way into the life of this couple from Nazareth forced to leave home in spite of the imminent birth of their child. On another level, however, Luke is showing that there is someone else who is *really* in control of the world's affairs. For Caesar's powerful decree ironically serves God's larger plan for the Messiah-King to be born in his proper city, Bethlehem.

Bethlehem had royal significance for the Jews. It was the city where David was born and was anointed king (see 1 Samuel 16:1-13). Most of all, Bethlehem had been associated with longings for the Messiah ever since the prophet Micah foretold that a new king would come to reunite the people of Israel and reign over all the nations. According to Micah, this new royal son, like David, would be born in Bethlehem:

> But you, O Bethlehem Ephrathah,
> who are little to be among the clans of Judah,
> from you shall come forth for me one who is to be ruler
>   in Israel,
> whose origin is from of old, from ancient days.
> —MICAH 5:2

In sum, from Luke's perspective, Caesar, in his own show of might with the worldwide census, unwittingly ends up serving the purposes of an even more powerful ruler, God himself. As a result of Caesar's decree, Mary and Joseph are brought to Bethlehem, and prophecy is fulfilled as a new king is born in the city of David.

The Firstborn Son

A few other points in this account are worth noting. First, Mary is described as Joseph's "betrothed." Since a betrothed woman in ancient Israel was someone married but not yet living with her husband (see Chapter Two), such a description for Mary at this stage in her life seems rather unusual, especially since she is traveling with Joseph and apparently living under the same roof. Luke probably calls Mary Joseph's "betrothed" in order to underscore her continued virginity at the time of Christ's birth. This would remind the reader that the newborn child came into the world not through natural means but through the power of the Holy Spirit (see 1:35).

Second, Luke describes Jesus as Mary's "first-born son" (see 2:7). This was a legal title associated with the special status given to the oldest son in ancient Israel. Luke's use of this title to describe Jesus does not suggest that Mary had other children after him but rather simply notes that Jesus held the important position of firstborn in his family. Luke makes this point to recall the rights of inheritance that the firstborn son held (see Deuteronomy 21:15-17).

What would Jesus inherit from his father Joseph? While Luke's Gospel does not tell us about Joseph's property, possessions or wealth, the one thing it does emphasize is his Davidic descent. In fact, here in the account of Jesus' birth, we read that Joseph travels to Bethlehem, "the city of *David*," precisely because he is "of the house and lineage of *David*" (2:4). Especially in this Davidic context, therefore, Jesus, as firstborn son, would be seen as inheriting Joseph's most valuable possession: his royal Davidic lineage.

This sheds light on a common question about Christ's claim to kingship: How can Jesus be a true descendant of David if he is not the physical son of Joseph? After all, since Jesus is only the adopted son of Joseph, he does not have the same royal blood as Joseph.

However, for ancient Jews adoption was not simply a contractual arrangement forming legal bonds between the man and the child. Adoption was covenantal, forming real family bonds between the two. The adopted child would be considered a true son and thus an heir. This is why ancient Jews would have no difficulty seeing Jesus as a true son of David. As the adopted son of Joseph, Jesus would inherit all that his father had to pass on—most especially his Davidic ancestry.

Why No Room?

A third point to consider is the location of Jesus' birth. Was Jesus born in a house, an inn, a stable or some other dwelling?

Luke's Gospel does not clearly settle this question. The only detail Luke offers is that Mary "laid him in a manger, because there was no place for them in the *katalyma*." Often translated "inn," the Greek word *katalyma* actually has a broader meaning, denoting any place of lodging. The word can refer to a guest room, a house, an inn or simply "a place to stay." It is best to translate this word simply as "lodging" to keep open the various possible settings in which Christ may have entered the world.

One possibility is that *katalyma* here refers to a travelers' inn, believed to be located near Bethlehem (see Jeremiah 41:17). Such an inn would have been very different from a modern motel with private living quarters and comfortable accommodations. A primitive Palestinian inn would have housed large groups of travelers under one roof, where guests would have slept on cots alongside the animals. In this view, Mary and Joseph could not find room in the travelers' inn, so they went somewhere else to have the baby.[1]

Another possibility is that *katalyma* refers to some type of guest room. Since Joseph is visiting his family's ancestral town, one might expect him to stay not at an inn for travelers but at the home of one of his relatives. In many peasant homes in ancient Palestine, family and animals slept in one enclosed space, with the family sleeping on a higher level and the animals residing below them. In this view, since there was no place to lay the baby in the presumably crowded sleeping quarters (*katalyma*), Mary put him in the manger, which would have been inside the home.

A third possibility is based on an early tradition, going back to the second century, which holds that Jesus was born in a cave on the outskirts of Bethlehem. This tradition was so strong that by A.D. 325 Constantine erected a basilica over a series of Bethlehem caves to commemorate the place where Jesus was believed to have been born. According to this view, there was no lodging within Bethlehem, so Joseph brought Mary to a cave near the village. This is at least plausible, since caves sometimes served as housing for Palestinian peasants and their animals.[2]

While the precise type of housing that sheltered Jesus at his birth may remain a mystery, the one thing Luke does make clear is that Israel's Messiah-King was born of humble origins. He arrived in a crowded living space, where the only place to lay him was in an animal's feeding trough.

With this in mind, think of the contrast between the two kings mentioned in this scene—Caesar and Jesus. The supposed king of the world, Caesar Augustus, flaunts his power by uprooting families throughout the empire so he can collect the Roman tax, while the true King of the world is born quietly in Bethlehem and placed in a manger, escaping the notice of most of the people he has come to save.

Interestingly, some early Christians saw in Christ's lowly beginnings a foreshadowing of his humiliating death. Just as Jesus at the start of his life was *wrapped* in bands of cloth and *laid* in a manger (see Luke 2:7), so at the end of his life he was *wrapped* in a linen cloth and *laid* in a tomb after being crucified on Calvary (see Luke 23:53). In fact, to express this connection, some Christian iconography later depicted Christ's birthplace as looking like a sepulcher.[3]

An Unusual Birth Announcement

> And in that region there were shepherds out in the field, keeping watch over their flock by night. And an angel of the Lord appeared to them, and the glory of the Lord shone around them, and they were filled with fear. And the angel said to them, "Be not afraid; for behold, I bring you good news of a great joy which will come to all the people; for to you is born this day in the city of David a Savior, who is Christ the Lord. And this will be a sign for you: you will find a babe wrapped in swaddling cloths and lying in a manger." And suddenly there was with the angel a multitude of the heavenly host praising God and saying,
>
> "Glory to God in the highest,
> and on earth peace among men with whom he is pleased!"
>
> —LUKE 2:8-14

Throughout the Bible, when God announces the birth of an important person, the account often includes the following four features: (1) an angel (or God himself) appears to one of the parents; (2) the parent responds in fear; (3) the birth is announced; and (4) a sign is given. We find this pattern generally followed in the three Old Testament birth annunciations—to Hagar (see Genesis 16:7-13), Abraham (see Genesis 17:1-21) and Manoah (Samson's mother) (see Judges 13:3-23)—and in Luke's accounts of the annunciation to Zechariah (see 1:11-20) and the annunciation to Mary (see 1:26-37).

Similarly, in this passage from Luke 2, when the birth of Jesus is announced to the shepherds, (1) the angel appears to the shepherds; (2) they respond in fear; (3) the angel announces the birth of the Messiah; and (4) the angel gives them the sign of the child wrapped in swaddling cloths and lying in a manger.

What is unusual, however, about this particular birth announcement is that it proclaims the birth of a child who is already born, rather than a child to be born in the future. Even more striking is the fact that in every other case in the Bible, angelic birth announcements are made *to the parents* of the coming child, never to people outside the family. For example, we never read of an angel appearing to a stranger and saying, "Go to the land of Canaan, and there you will find a woman named Sarah who in her old age has given birth to a son named Isaac." Birth announcements were kept in the family.

However, when the angel of the Lord announces Jesus' birth in Bethlehem, he announces it to shepherds out in a field—to a group of people who don't have any relationship to Mary and Joseph. In fact, they are complete strangers! This open, public proclamation of Christ's birth underscores the child's universal mission. The baby Jesus will bring blessing not just to his parents. In the words of the angel, this child also will be "a great joy" for "*all* the people."

A Night to Remember

Imagine what these shepherds experienced on that first Christmas. In the midst of keeping their sheep during the night watch in the Bethlehem countryside, an angel of the Lord appears in the darkness, and they suddenly find themselves encircled by "the glory of the Lord."

In the Old Testament God's "glory" was the visible manifestation of his divine presence. It often appeared in the form of a cloud, and it was associated with God's presence covering the ark of the covenant and filling the Holy of Holies of the temple in Jerusalem (see Exodus 40:34; 1 Kings 8:11; Ezekiel 10:4, 18). Now this same divine glory appears in an open field to these simple, lowly shepherds. No wonder they respond in fear! The splendid display of God's glory illuminates the night, shining around the shepherds in ways reminiscent of Zechariah's song, which foretold that the Messiah would "give light to those who sit in darkness" (1:79).

After this startling greeting, the angel delivers his message: On this very day, in the city of David, the long-awaited "Christ"—Israel's Messiah-King—has been born! At this moment these shepherds become the first in all of Israel to learn about the Messiah's birth.

Once the announcement is made, this single angel is joined by a great multitude of angels who are praising God: "Glory to God in the highest, and on earth peace among men with whom he is well pleased." Here we have the third and shortest of the canticles in Luke's infancy narrative. As with the other canticles, we readers are invited to join in the praise of God for sending the world its Savior.

This time, however, the praise is sung at a much higher level. It is no longer just human beings like Mary and Zechariah glorifying the Lord. Now God's own royal entourage, a multitude of angels from the countless "heavenly hosts," joins the act. They bring their chorus of praise from God's throne in heaven down to the fields of Bethlehem in order to welcome the birth of the Messiah.

From the Bottom to the Top

> When the angels went away from them into heaven, the shepherds said to one another, "Let us go over to Bethlehem and see this thing that has happened, which the Lord has made known to us." And they went with haste, and found Mary and Joseph,

and the babe lying in a manger. And when they saw it they made known the saying which had been told them concerning this child; and all who heard it wondered at what the shepherds told them. But Mary kept all these things, pondering them in her heart. And the shepherds returned, glorifying and praising God for all they had heard and seen, as it had been told them.

—LUKE 2:15-20

The shepherds have been completely transformed by this experience. As Mary responded to Gabriel's message, so they respond to the angel's message "with haste" (see 1:39; 2:16). They find the child lying in the manger and cannot help but praise God and then go tell others of their encounter with him. Thus the shepherds become the first evangelists in Luke's Gospel. And this is astonishing: The first people to proclaim the Messiah's arrival are not the Jewish priests, Pharisees or other religious leaders of the day but these lowly shepherds in the Bethlehem countryside!

This is not the first time God has shown extraordinary favor to shepherds. In the Old Testament, people like Jacob, Joseph, Moses and Amos were shepherds whom God called to a special role of service for his people.

The most famous shepherd of all, however, was King David. As a boy David tended sheep (see 1 Samuel 16:11). After Yahweh raised him up to be king over Israel, he was told he would "shepherd" God's people, the twelve tribes of Israel (see 2 Samuel 5:2). This is why shepherd imagery became associated with the Davidic dynasty and the hopes for a Messiah-King. For example, the prophet Ezekiel describes how in the new covenant the people will be reunited around a new son of David, like sheep gathering around their shepherd: "And I will set up over them *one shepherd*, my servant *David*, and he shall feed them; he shall lead them and be their shepherd" (Ezekiel 34:23, emphasis added).

With this background in mind, *shepherds* coming to *Bethlehem, the city of David*, to meet the newborn *Christ* heighten the royal Davidic character of Jesus' birth. Now this group of Bethlehem shepherds gathers around the one true shepherd, the new David, who will lead the flock of Israel back to Yahweh.

Front Row Seats

The shepherds' role in Luke's narrative can be appreciated even more when we consider how shepherds were viewed in first-century Judaism. Often working for other land owners, shepherds received low wages and had little social status. They would have been considered part of "the poor," not simply for their economic situation but also because some circles of Jews considered them dishonest and outside of God's covenant.[4]

In light of this social context, it is astonishing that God chooses to first reveal the Messiah not to the religious leaders in Jerusalem nor to the political rulers in Herod's palace but to these shepherds in the fields. The theme of reversal announced in Mary's song resounds this night in Bethlehem. The birth of the Messiah escapes the notice of the powerful and privileged in Israel, while lowly shepherds in their ordinary labor have front row seats to the glory of God and the birth of the King who will change the world.

Reflection Questions

1. In the first century Caesar was hailed as the "savior of the world" and "son of God" who brought "good news" of peace throughout the world. His birthday was celebrated as a feast throughout the empire. How does Luke's account

of Christ's birth subvert this pagan propaganda of the Roman empire?

2.   Since Christ is divine, he is the only baby in the world to be able to choose where he wanted to be born. Yet he chose to enter this world in conditions of extreme poverty, with rough accommodations, even being laid in a manger. Commenting on this theme, the *Catechism of the Catholic Church* (#525), says, "In this poverty heaven's glory was made manifest." How does God's glory contrast with the world's understanding of glory? Which do you seek? In what ways might the glory of the world distract you from pursuing the glory of God with all your heart?

3.   Put yourself in Mary's shoes. She is the Immaculate Conception and the mother of the Messiah-King. Yet, near the end of her pregnancy, she is forced to leave her home, travel far to the south and give birth to her child in conditions of poverty in the unfamiliar town of Bethlehem. Nowhere do we read of Mary's complaining or requesting better accommodations. She never demands royal treatment ("I'm the mother of the Messiah!").

  ✳ What can you learn from Mary's example?

  ✳ How can you respond when you don't get what you think you deserve? How can you respond virtuously to poor treatment at a business, in your parish, from your boss or from a family member?

4. Why is it significant that Christ was born in Bethlehem?

    * First, consider the prophecy of Micah 5:2.

    * Second, consider the meaning of the word "Bethlehem" ("House of Bread"). (See John 6:36 and *Catechism of the Catholic Church*, #1374-1375.) What parallels are there between the way the Son of God manifested himself to the world in Bethlehem and the ways he presents himself to us today in the Bread of Life, the Eucharist?

5. How were shepherds viewed in the time of Christ? Why is it surprising that they were the first to welcome the Messiah? How might this relate to what Mary said in Luke 1:50-53?

6. How do you regard those in your own family, parish, work place or community who (like the shepherds) don't seem to fit in socially? In what ways might God use them to bring "good news" to us?

Chapter Six

Pierced by a Sword
The Presentation
(Luke 2:21-40)

And at the end of eight days, when he was circumcised, he was called Jesus, the name given by the angel before he was conceived in the womb. And when the time came for their purification according to the law of Moses, they brought him up to Jerusalem to present him to the Lord (as it is written in the law of the Lord, "Every male that opens the womb shall be called holy to the Lord") and to offer a sacrifice according to what is said in the law of the Lord, "a pair of turtledoves, or two young pigeons."

—Luke 2:21-24

Forty days after his birth in Bethlehem, the Son of God is brought to the Jerusalem temple. Keep in mind that this is *his* temple—the house of the living God. Still, Jesus' entry into this most sacred building escapes the notice of most of the other pilgrims that day. He comes not in royal splendor but humbly as a child. And like everyone else, he comes as one under the Law.

In fact, it is the Jewish law that brings him to the house of God. Let us consider the two important Jewish customs in the background of this scene: the purification of the mother and the presentation of the firstborn son.

Two Turtledoves

After giving birth to a male child, a Jewish mother was considered ritually impure for forty days. During this period she was not allowed to enter the temple. When her forty days of purification were completed, she was to offer a lamb and a young pigeon to the priests at the sanctuary. If a woman could not afford a lamb, she could present two young pigeons or doves instead (see Leviticus 12:1-8).

This background tells us something important about Mary and Joseph. The fact that they offer "a pair of turtledoves or two young pigeons" (2:24) indicates that they are poor; they cannot afford a lamb for the sacrifice. Nevertheless, they have something much more valuable to present to God. As John Paul II has pointed out, they bring to the temple "the true Lamb," the child Jesus, who will redeem humanity through his sacrifice on the cross.[1]

The second ritual is the presentation of the firstborn son. In the previous chapter we saw how firstborn sons possessed the right of inheritance. Originally, however, their position in the family held even greater importance. In the Book of Genesis and the first part of the Book of Exodus, firstborn sons were consecrated to Yahweh. They not only received an inheritance, but they also were set apart to serve the Lord and carry out priestly duties (see Exodus 13:1-2). However, after Israel's act of idolatry in worshipping the golden calf on Mount Sinai, this priestly role was stripped from the firstborn sons and given to the only tribe who remained faithful to Yahweh that day, the Levites (see Exodus 32:29; Numbers 3:11-13; 8:14-19).

Since the firstborn originally were meant to be consecrated, Jewish law required them to be "bought back" so they could be released from their special service to the Lord. The price of five shekels was paid to the temple to support the ones who replaced them, the Levitical priests (see Numbers 18:15-16).[2] As a first-born son from a non-priestly family, Jesus submits to the law of Moses. Mary and Joseph present him to the temple priests to be bought back from traditional Jewish priestly duty.

"Comfort, Comfort My People"

> Now there was a man in Jerusalem, whose name was Simeon, and this man was righteous and devout, looking for the consolation of Israel, and the Holy Spirit was upon him. And it had been revealed to him by the Holy Spirit that he should not see death before he had seen the Lord's Christ. And inspired by the Spirit he came into the temple; and when the parents brought in the child Jesus, to do for him according to the custom of the law, he took him up in his arms and blessed God....
>
> —LUKE 2:25-28

When entering the temple, Mary and Joseph encounter a man who has been waiting his entire life to see the child Jesus. The man's name is Simeon. He is a "righteous and devout" Jew and Luke portrays him as a prophet filled with the Holy Spirit. Even more, Simeon has received an extraordinary revelation from the Holy Spirit that he will not die before seeing the Lord's Messiah.

Perhaps the most interesting detail about Simeon, however, is that he is looking for "the *consolation* of Israel"—an important theme from the Book of Isaiah. This phrase brings to mind what every first-century Jew would be yearning for: the fulfillment of Isaiah's prophecies about God's consoling Israel and bringing an end to their sufferings under the pagan nations (see Isaiah 40:1; 49:13; 51:3; 52:9; 57:18; 66:10-11).

This theme of consolation plays such an important role in Isaiah that biblical scholars often use it to characterize the last twenty-seven chapters of the book. The first part of Isaiah (chapters 1–39) is commonly called "the Book of Judgment" because much of its focus is on warning Israel that God will come in judgment for their sins. The second part (chapters 40–66) is commonly called "the Book of Consolation" because it announces God's mercy and forgiveness. In these later chapters Isaiah announces that the period of judgment will not last forever. God eventually will console his people in their sufferings, bring an end to their punishments and forgive their sins.

What is important for us to note is that Isaiah begins his entire section of good news in chapter 40 with this very message of Israel's consolation: "Comfort, comfort my people, says your God. Speak tenderly to Jerusalem, and cry to her that her warfare is ended, that her iniquity is pardoned" (Isaiah 40:1-2). This announcement of consolation (or comfort) thus serves as the hinge between the "bad news" and the "good news" in the Book of Isaiah. And it is precisely this turning point that Luke's Gospel brings to mind when it describes Simeon as waiting for "the consolation of Israel."

Therefore, Simeon, at the twilight of his life, still awaits the fulfillment of the second part of Isaiah's prophecies. Luke thus presents Simeon as a model Jew who, in his own desire to see the Messiah, represents the hopes of all the faithful Jewish people who long for God to console them and bring about the good news of Isaiah 40–66.

The Encounter of a Lifetime

Then one day it finally happens. While visiting the temple under the inspiration of the Holy Spirit, Simeon encounters Mary and Joseph carrying the child he has been waiting all his life to see. What a moment this must be for Simeon! He holds the infant Jesus in his arms and breaks out in praise of God, saying:

> Lord, now lettest thou thy servant depart in peace,
> according to thy word;
> for mine eyes have seen thy salvation
> which thou hast prepared in the presence of all peoples,
> a light for revelation to the Gentiles,
> and for glory to thy people Israel.
>
> —LUKE 2:29-32

These verses, commonly known as the *Nunc Dimittis*, represent the fourth canticle in Luke's Gospel. Like the others, this hymn-like praise of God gives the reader a chance to reflect on the mystery of this newborn child and the significance of his mission here on earth.

If we were first-century Jews in the temple that day, we would hear Simeon proclaiming the Christ child to be the fulfillment of all our hopes and expectations. For example, Simeon calls Jesus "a light of revelation to the Gentiles." This image would bring to mind yet another major theme from the Book of Isaiah: *the servant of the Lord*.

According to Isaiah 41–49, God called Israel to be his servant (see Isaiah 41:8) and gave her the mission to evangelize the pagan nations: "I have given you as a covenant to the people, *a light to the nations*, to open the eyes that are blind" (Isaiah 42:6-7, emphasis added). However, because of her own sinfulness, Israel became blind, and she herself needed to be led back on track (see 42:18-22). Isaiah foretold that consequently God would send his own servant to restore the people of Israel and to fulfill their mission to the Gentiles. Addressing this future servant of the Lord, God says:

> …you should be my servant to raise up the tribes of Jacob and to restore the preserved of Israel; I will give you as *a light to the nations*, that my salvation may reach to the end of the earth.
> —ISAIAH 49:6, emphasis added

When Simeon calls the child "a light for revelation to the Gentiles," he announces that Jesus is this servant of the Lord from Isaiah. Jesus thus will do what Israel was always meant to do: be light to the world and gather all nations back into God's covenant family.

The Glory of the Lord

Another image that Simeon brings to our attention is *the glory of the Lord*. Simeon proclaims the Christ child to be "glory" for the people of Israel.

We already have seen in Chapter Five that *glory* was the word used to describe God's manifestation of his holy presence, especially over the ark of the covenant and in the temple. For example, at Mount Sinai God's glory covered the ark and filled the sanctuary in the form of a cloud (see Exodus 40:34). When Solomon dedicated the temple in Jerusalem, "the glory of the LORD filled the house of the LORD" (1 Kings 8:11). When the prophet Ezekiel received a vision of the temple, he saw it filled with "the glory of the LORD" and fell on his face in worship (see Ezekiel 44:4).

However, God's glory did not remain in the temple forever. Babylon conquered Jerusalem, destroyed the temple and carried the people away in exile in 586 B.C. Shortly before the Babylonian invasion, Ezekiel was given a vision in which God's glory left the temple and the city of Jerusalem because of the people's unfaithfulness (see Ezekiel 10–11). This would have been an ominous sign of the impending judgment upon the holy city.

In this same time period, another prophet named Jeremiah hid the ark of the covenant in a cave to protect it from desecration by the invading Babylonians. He said it would not be found until the day when God gathers his people together again (see 2 Maccabees 2:4-8).

Consequently, even though the Jews returned to Jerusalem in 515 B.C. and rebuilt the temple, they would have realized that things were not the same. The new temple did not house God's presence as it had done in the days of old. Although standing on holy ground and serving as the center of Jewish worship, the new temple still was missing its most sacred items: the ark of the covenant and "the glory of the Lord." Thus, for hundreds of years the Jews were longing for God's glory-presence to be with them again in the temple.[3]

With this background in mind, we can see that when Simeon stands within the barren temple of the Lord and calls the infant Jesus "a light…for glory to thy people Israel," he is saying a lot. God's glory-presence, which has not been with the people for over five hundred years, has finally returned to the temple! But this time it appears not in the form of a cloud, but in the presence of this little child. As one Scripture scholar has commented, "It was the proudest boast of the Temple theologians that the glory of God dwelt in the sanctuary (1 Kings 8:10-11; Ezekiel 44:4); and now as Simeon stands before that sanctuary, he proclaims Jesus to be a glory for God's people Israel."[4]

Fittingly, it is Mary who has brought Jesus to the temple in this scene. We already have seen how Luke's Gospel portrays Mary as the new ark of the covenant, bearing God's presence (see chapter 3). Like the ark of old, Mary now carries the God-man to Jerusalem and restores the glory of the Lord to the temple.

Seventy Weeks of Years

We also can see this theme of God's presence returning to the temple in one of the prophet Daniel's famous visions, which serves as an important backdrop for Luke's Gospel.

Daniel was a Jewish man who grew up in Babylon during the period of Israel's exile. In fact, seventy years had passed since the Babylonians destroyed the Jerusalem temple and carried the people off into slavery. Thus, for seventy years the temple was desolate, abandoned by God and lying in ruins, while the Jewish people were enslaved in a foreign land hundreds of miles from home.

Daniel pleaded with God to free the Jews from their pagan oppressors. In the midst of this prayer he asked God to restore the temple: "O Lord, cause thy face to shine upon thy sanctuary, which is desolate" (Daniel 9:17). In response, God sent the angel Gabriel to give Daniel a prophecy that would give hope for the Jews for ages to come.

At the hour of the evening sacrifice, Gabriel appeared to Daniel and announced that God would answer his prayer but only after a long period of time—a period described as "seventy weeks of years" (Daniel 9:24). In that time God would send "an anointed one" (*messiah*) who would do great things. He would bring an end to sin, atone for iniquity, usher in everlasting righteousness, fulfill all prophecy and anoint a Holy of Holies (see Daniel 9:24-27).

While most interpreters conclude that the "seventy weeks of years" is symbolic of 490 years (since "a week" of years would symbolize seven years, and 70 x 7 years = 490 years), the main point of Gabriel's message is that it will be several centuries before God sends his Messiah to restore the Jewish people and shine his face again on the holy temple.

The next time the angel Gabriel appears in the Bible is hundreds of years later in the annunciation to Zechariah. And his appearance to Zechariah parallels the way he appeared to Daniel, as I detailed in Chapter Four. Just as *Gabriel* appeared to Daniel *in response to his prayer* at the *hour of the temple sacrifice* to announce the "seventy weeks of years," so the same *Gabriel* visited Zechariah *in response to his prayer* at the *hour of the temple sacrifice* to announce the dawn of the new covenant.

Gabriel's return in such a similar manner after several centuries of silence signals the end of Israel's "seventy weeks of years" of suffering under the pagans. It shows the arrival of the new era, which will finally answer Daniel's prayer for God's face to shine again in the sanctuary—the age when sin will be atoned for, prophecy will be fulfilled and the Holy of Holies will be anointed.[5]

All this is important because the chronology of Luke's narrative subtly expresses the fulfillment of Daniel's "seventy weeks of years" by offering a 490-day period, which begins and ends in the temple. Luke's Gospel begins with Gabriel's announcement to

Zechariah in the temple and reaches a significant climax 490 days later in the scene, the presentation of Jesus in the temple.[6]

After Gabriel announces the conception of John the Baptist and the beginning of the new era, we are told that Elizabeth kept her conception hidden for five months (see Luke 1:24). In the sixth month of her pregnancy, the angel Gabriel appeared to Mary and she conceived Jesus (see 1:26). Since a month was thirty days for the Jews, Mary's conceiving Jesus in the sixth month of Elizabeth's pregnancy would indicate that Jesus was conceived about 180 days after Gabriel appeared to Zechariah (6 months x 30 days = 180 days). Furthermore, Mary would have been pregnant for nine months, which is 270 days (9 months x 30 days = 270 days). Therefore, Jesus would have been born on the 450th day after Gabriel's visit to Zechariah (180 days + 270 days = 450 days).

Finally, since the purification of the mother took place forty days after the birth of a male child, Mary would have presented Jesus in the temple on the 490th day. Thus we can see that 490 days after Gabriel appeared to Zechariah to signal the end of Daniel's "seventy weeks of years," God's glory-presence returns to the temple in the infant Jesus. Daniel's plea for God's face to shine in the sanctuary is finally answered in the presentation scene. The temple is anointed by the presence of God in the Messiah, echoing Gabriel's message in Daniel.

The 490 Days

Day 1	Elizabeth conceives John the Baptist.
Day 180	Mary conceives Jesus in the sixth month of Elizabeth's pregnancy (180 days later).

| Day 450 | Jesus is born nine months (or 270 days) later. |
| Day 490 | Jesus is presented in the temple forty days after his birth. |

"A Sword Will Pierce Through Your Own Soul"

> And his father and his mother marveled at what was said about
> him; and Simeon blessed them and said to Mary his mother,
> "Behold, this child is set for the fall
> and rising of many in Israel,
> and for a sign that is spoken against
> (and a sword will pierce through your own soul also),
> that thoughts out of many hearts may be revealed."
> —LUKE 2:33-35

These words represent a second oracle from Simeon. In his first oracle Simeon joyfully proclaimed Christ to be a light of revelation to the Gentiles and glory to his people Israel. Now the joy that radiates in this scene suddenly turns to sorrow. In a prophecy addressed specifically to Mary, Simeon looks at her and warns her of the difficult path that lies ahead.

First Simeon says that Mary's son will bring about "the fall and rising of many in Israel." These words echo the theme of reversal announced in Mary's song: The lowly will be exalted, while the mighty will be cast down (see 1:51-54). They foreshadow the fact that through Christ's public ministry, many of the poor, the Gentiles and other covenant outsiders will be raised up and included in Christ's kingdom. On the other hand, many of the religious and political leaders of the Jews will oppose Jesus. They will be cast down, for they will not accept the kingdom he offers them.

Simeon also says that Jesus will be "a sign that is *spoken against*" (emphasis added). In Luke's writing, this particular Greek word for being "spoken against," *antilegomenon*, is used to describe not just any form of opposition but specifically *Jewish* opposition to Jesus (see Luke 20:27; 21:15; Acts 4:14; 13:45; 28:19-22).[7]

Now we begin to see how Simeon's two oracles relate to each other. In the first, Simeon rejoices in Jesus' being "a light of revelation to the nations." However, it is this very theme of gathering in the lost that will get Jesus into trouble. He will be criticized by the Pharisees, chief priests and others for including all the "wrong people" in his ministry—the sinners, the Gentiles and other outcasts (see, for example, Luke 5:29-32; 15:1-2). Thus the Jewish leaders' opposition to Christ (the theme of the second oracle) is the result of his mission to be light to those in darkness (the theme of the first oracle).

"A Second Annunciation"

The intensity of this opposition is depicted by the sword imagery of verse 35: "A sword will pierce through your own soul also." These words tell Mary two things.

First, a sword will pierce her son. In the Old Testament the sword symbolized bloodshed, death and war (see, for example, Genesis 27:40; Leviticus 26:6; Deuteronomy 32:25; Joshua 5:13; Isaiah 1:20). The image of a sword piercing Jesus points to the violent hostility he will face when challenging Israel to be the light to the world. Simeon's words foreshadow the fact that Jesus' ministry will culminate in his bloody death on the cross. There, in fact, a Roman soldier will pierce his side with a sword (see John 19:34).

The second thing these words tell Mary is that the intense opposition to Jesus will affect *her* as well: "A sword will pierce *your soul also.*" Here we have a foreshadowing of the suffering Mary will endure in watching her own son die on the cross. John Paul II once described Simeon's words as "a second annunciation to Mary": "[These words] tell her of the actual historical situation in which the Son is to accomplish his mission, namely, in misunderstanding and sorrow.... [Simeon] also reveals to her that she will have to live her obedience of faith in suffering, at the side of the suffering Savior, and that her motherhood will be mysterious and sorrowful."[8]

Indeed, here at the presentation Mary receives a fuller picture of what she signed up for when she first consented to serve as the mother of the Messiah at the Annunciation. Now, almost a year later, she gains a fuller understanding of just how challenging this vocation will be. In fact, her *fiat* in Galilee, where she first accepted the life of the Christ child in her womb, ultimately will lead her to Calvary, where she sorrowfully will witness the offering of his life on the cross.

Simeon and Anna

> And there was a prophetess Anna, the daughter of Phanuel, of the tribe of Asher; she was of a great age, having lived with her husband seven years from her virginity, and as a widow till she was eighty-four. She did not depart from the temple, worshiping with fasting and prayer night and day. And coming up at that very hour she gave thanks to God, and spoke of him to all who were looking for the redemption of Jerusalem. And when they had performed everything according to the law of the Lord, they returned into Galilee, to their own city, Nazareth. And the child grew and became strong, filled with wisdom; and the favor of God was upon him.
>
> —LUKE 2:36-40

We do not have a lot of information about Anna. She is a prophetess who was married for seven years, and after her husband's death she remained a widow. Although verse 37 in the *RSV* translation says she was a widow "till she was eighty-four" (implying she was eighty-four years old in this scene), the Greek used in this verse also can mean that she remained a widow for eighty-four years *after* her marriage.[9] If that is the case, Anna probably would be about 105, assuming she was married at about fourteen, a common age for marriage in those days.

Like Simeon, Anna in her old age is awaiting the time when God will act in history to bring about the redemption of Israel. She dedicates herself to fasting and worship in the temple day and night. Through these pious practices Anna expresses the hope that God will soon set things right for her people. And finally, on this particular day, as Simeon is holding Jesus in his arms, Anna lays her eyes on the child and joins Simeon in giving thanks to God for sending the Messiah to Israel.

The little we know about the prophetess Anna might remind us of the Jewish heroine Judith, whom God used to rescue his people from a Babylonian general. Like Anna, Judith was a widow who did not remarry and dedicated herself to fasting and obeying the Law (see Judith 8:1-8). Like Anna, who gives thanks to God after seeing the Messiah, Judith sang a canticle of thanksgiving after Israel was delivered from the pagans (see Judith 16:1-17). And just as Anna lived to an old age, so did Judith live to be 105 (see Judith 16:23).

Priest, Prophet and King

Together Simeon and Anna play an important role in the presentation. Both are old, and both have waited a long time for God to redeem Israel. Anna has been praying and fasting, awaiting the redemption of Israel, while Simeon knows he will not die until he sees the Messiah himself. In their old age and in their yearnings for the Messiah to come, Simeon and Anna represent the long history of God's people who have been waiting for God to act in their lives. Thus, the rejoicing and thanksgiving of these two prophets who finally encounter Christ anticipates the many in Israel who soon will have their hopes fulfilled and be blessed to know their Messiah. As the *Catechism of the Catholic Church* explains, "With Simeon and Anna, all Israel awaits its *encounter* with the Savior" (#529).

Finally, Simeon and Anna represent the third male-female pair in Luke's Gospel. What is interesting is that each pair not only plays a key role in announcing Jesus' mission but also represents one of the three offices of Jesus: priest, prophet and king. Zechariah and Elizabeth are a *priestly* family. Joseph and Mary are a *kingly* family, coming from the house of David. And Simeon and Anna are *prophets*. Thus the three male-female pairs involved in the mission of the Messiah so far represent his three principle offices of priest, prophet and king.[10]

Reflection Questions

1. Read Luke 2:22-24. Explain the two Jewish customs in the background of this scene, the presentation of the firstborn and the purification of the mother.

2. Luke 2:24 tells us that Mary and Joseph offer a "pair of turtledoves or young pigeons" when they present Jesus to the temple. What does this fact tell us about the Holy

Family (see Leviticus 12:8)? What was the real treasure they brought to the temple?

3. Read Luke 2:25-28. Simeon waited his whole life to see the Messiah. According to verse 27, why did Simeon decide to go to the temple at the moment Mary and Joseph were bringing Jesus there? What would have happened if Simeon hadn't followed the prompting of the Holy Spirit that day?

   ✳ Describe a time when you sensed that God was prompting you to do something. What was the result of your following that prompting?

   ✳ In what ways is God prompting you now? What might he be asking you to do?

4. What does God's "glory" refer to in the Old Testament? See Exodus 40:34; 1 Kings 8:10-11; Ezekiel 44:4.

5. In light of Jewish beliefs about God's presence in the temple, what is the significance of Jesus' entering the temple and being called "glory" by Simeon in Luke 2:32?

6. Simeon's second prophecy is addressed to Mary (see Luke 2:33-35). What is the meaning of the following three statements Simeon makes about Christ's future?

   ✳ He is set for "the fall and rising of many in Israel" (2:34).

   ✳ He will be "a sign that is spoken against" (2:34).

   ✳ "A sword will pierce" him (2:35; see also John 19:34).

7. Luke 2:35 says "a sword will pierce" Mary also. What does this tell us about Mary's future (see John 19:25-27)?

8. Luke does not tell us Mary's response to Simeon's words. From what you can learn elsewhere of Mary (see Luke 1:38; 2:19, 51; John 14:25-27), how do you think she responded?

9. Simeon and Anna in their old age patiently wait for the Lord to send the Messiah and rescue Israel. What did Anna do while waiting for God to act (see Luke 2:36-37)? How is Simeon described in his waiting for the Messiah (2:25)?

10. Describe a situation in which you have been waiting a long time for something to change and for God to set things right. How might the example of Simeon and Anna inspire you and give you hope?

CHAPTER SEVEN

In His Father's House
The Finding of Jesus in the Temple
(Luke 2:41-52)

> Now his parents went to Jerusalem every year at the feast of the
> Passover. And when he was twelve years old, they went up
> according to custom; and when the feast was ended, as they
> were returning, the boy Jesus stayed behind in Jerusalem. His
> parents did not know it, but supposing him to be in the com-
> pany they went a day's journey, and they sought him among
> their kinsfolk and acquaintances; and when they did not find
> him, they returned to Jerusalem, seeking him.
>
> —LUKE 2:41-45

AT FIRST GLANCE THIS story is shocking. How could Mary and
Joseph forget their son and leave him behind in the large city of
Jerusalem? What kind of parents would do such a thing? Looking
at this account apart from its historical context, we might be
tempted to view Mary and Joseph as irresponsible parents.
However, a closer look may help us see their dilemma with a little
more understanding.

Passover was one of the annual feasts for which many Jews
made a pilgrimage to Jerusalem to worship at the temple. On

these journeys people often traveled in large caravans in order to share resources and to have greater security. Especially for pilgrims from the northern region of Galilee who journeyed south to Jerusalem, large travel groups offered protection from bandits along the roadways. These pilgrims would also pass through the land of the Samaritans, who would not have been hospitable to the Jews.[1]

Such a caravan of families would have been large and rather chaotic. Since extended family often shared responsibility for the children, it would not be surprising for parents to assume that their fellow kinsmen were looking after their child. That seems to be what happened in this scene: "Supposing him to be in the company [that is, the caravan] they went a day's journey, and they sought him among their kinsfolk and acquaintances." Not finding him among their friends and relatives, Mary and Joseph headed back to Jerusalem in search of their lost son.

A Beautiful Mind

> After three days they found him in the temple, sitting among the teachers, listening to them and asking them questions; and all who heard him were amazed at his understanding and his answers. And when they saw him they were astonished; and his mother said to him, "Son, why have you treated us so? Behold, your father and I have been looking for you anxiously." And he said to them, "How is it that you sought me? Did you not know that I must be in my Father's house?" And they did not understand the saying which he spoke to them. And he went down with them and came to Nazareth, and was obedient to them; and his mother kept all these things in her heart. And Jesus increased in wisdom and in stature, and in favor with God and man.
>
> —LUKE 2:46-52

The picture painted in verse 46 is just what we should expect: a young Jewish boy listening to his elders in the temple and asking them questions. What is surprising, however, is the following verse: "And all who heard him were amazed at his understanding and his answers." For a Jewish child to astonish his elder teachers in the temple with his own insights would have been extraordinary. Luke thus presents Jesus as having phenomenal understanding even at a young age.

This scene in the temple foreshadows Jesus' adult life. In the years to come, many will be amazed at his powerful teachings. In particular the scene points forward to Christ's dramatic return to the temple during the last week of his life, when he will amaze the people once again with his wisdom and his teaching (see Luke 19:45–21:38).

On finding Jesus in the temple, Mary and Joseph are astonished as well, but for different reasons. Mary asks Jesus how he could have treated his parents this way: "Your father and I have been looking for you anxiously." Jesus responds, "How is it that you sought me? Did you not know that I must be in my Father's house?"

These words need not be interpreted as a rebuke of his parents. After all, the narrative goes on to highlight that Jesus submits to their authority, leaves the temple and returns to their home in Nazareth, where he remains obedient to them. Instead his words seem to be more of surprise ("How is it that you sought me?") and instruction ("Did you not know that I must be in my Father's house?").

In one sense Jesus' speaking of his heavenly Father's house refers to the actual place where they find him, the temple of God, which was commonly known as God's house. The expression, however, also could be translated as his "Father's affairs" or his

"Father's business." Since "household" in the ancient Greco-Roman world could denote not only a place but also a family authority, it is likely that both these meanings come into play here.[2]

What is most important is the contrast between "your father" and "my Father" in this dialogue. Mary speaks of Christ's human parents: "*Your* father and I have been looking for you anxiously." Christ responds by saying he must be concentrating on the affairs of his *heavenly* Father: "I must be in *my* Father's house." While he will always honor his human parents, Jesus reminds them of his primary allegiance to his heavenly Father's saving plan. He must be about his Father's affairs. And this desire to fulfill his heavenly Father's will may cause his human parents great grief and anxiety at times, as it has during these three days.

Preview of the Passion

The finding of Jesus in the temple is the only account we have about Christ's "hidden years." From the time when Jesus was a forty-day-old infant being presented in the temple to the time he was baptized in the Jordan as a thirty-year-old adult, this scene is the only biblical record we have of Christ's youth. Why is this one scene so important? Why was this the only story from Christ's youth deemed weighty enough to be included in the Gospel?

Within the wider context of Luke's narrative, this scene serves as a crucial bridge connecting Christ's infancy to his public ministry as an adult. On one hand, it serves as an initial fulfillment of Simeon's prophecy to Mary about the suffering she will endure as a result of her son's mission: "A sword will pierce your own soul also" (2:35). When the twelve-year-old Christ is lost in Jerusalem, Mary already begins to experience these pains. She suffers the loss of her son for three days as he is busy conducting his Father's affairs.

On the other hand, this initial suffering of Mary is a fore-taste of the bitter pains she will endure in the future, for this scene prefigures what will happen when Jesus follows his heavenly Father's will all the way to the cross. Consider what takes place in this present story: Jesus makes a pilgrimage from Galilee to Jerusalem to celebrate the Passover. He enters the temple and amazes the people with his wisdom. While in Jerusalem he is lost, and this causes his mother great suffering. On the third day the child Jesus is found again.

All this "pre-enacts" what will take place at the end of Jesus' life. At the culmination of his public ministry, Jesus will make one last pilgrimage from Galilee to Jerusalem for the feast of Passover. Once again he will enter the temple and amaze the people with his teaching. And Mary will lose her son again, but this time in an even more profound way as he is crucified on Calvary. However, just as in his youth, Jesus will be found on the third day when he rises from the dead.

The *Catechism of the Catholic Church* notes how Mary pondered this experience from her son's childhood in her heart:

> The *finding of Jesus in the temple* is the only event that breaks the silence of the Gospels about the hidden years of Jesus. Here Jesus lets us catch a glimpse of the mystery of his total consecration to a mission that flows from his divine sonship: "Did you not know that I must be about my Father's work?" Mary and Joseph did not understand these words, but they accepted them in faith. Mary "kept all these things in her heart" during the years Jesus remained hidden in the silence of an ordinary life. (#534)

Increased in Wisdom?

Luke closes his infancy narrative by telling us that Jesus "increased in wisdom" (2:52). This passage has bewildered many Christians for obvious reasons. If we believe Jesus is God, and God knows everything, how could Jesus *grow* in wisdom and still be God? Does God learn something he did not know before?

The classical distinctions between Christ's types of knowledge will be helpful here. First, Jesus had what is known as "beatific knowledge"—direct vision of the Father by virtue of his human nature being united to his divine person. "The human nature of God's Son, *not by itself but by its union with the Word*, knew and showed forth in itself everything that pertains to God" (*Catechism of the Catholic Church*, #473). Thus, on one level, Jesus, even in his human nature, knew everything by virtue of its union with his divine person.

Yet, at the same time, Christ is said to have had "acquired" or "experiential" knowledge. This type of knowledge refers to how the Son, the divine Person who already knows everything from all eternity, comes to know some of these things in a new way, that is, in a human nature. Thus, Christ's "acquired knowledge" does not refer to new *content* that the Son comes to know for the first time. Rather, it refers to a new *mode* by which the Son comes to know the truths that he knows from all eternity.

In other words, when the Son assumes human nature, he comes to know things in a new way, in a human fashion— through the human senses and in a gradual progression, applying human reason. Thus, when Luke's Gospel speaks of Jesus' growing in wisdom, this may be best understood in terms of the new mode of knowledge that Christ acquired in assuming a human nature. As the *Catechism* explains, "This is why the Son of God could, when he became man, 'increase in wisdom and in stature, and in favor with God and man,' and would even have *to inquire for himself about what one in the human condition can learn only from experience*" (#472, emphasis added).

Reflection Questions

1. How could Mary and Joseph leave their son behind in the big city of Jerusalem? Are they irresponsible parents? Explain.

2. Apart from his infancy, this scene of the twelve-year-old Christ being lost and found in the temple is the only account we have of his childhood in the entire New Testament.

    * Why do you think Luke includes this particular scene?

    * Consider how this scene relates to what Simeon said to Mary in the presentation scene (see Luke 2:25).

    * In what ways does this scene anticipate the climax of Christ's public ministry?

3. Consider Mary's words to Jesus and his response in 2:48-49. Is Jesus rebuking his parents? What does he mean when he speaks of needing to be in his "Father's house"? Describe a situation in which you were trying to do what God wants but family or friends did not understand.

4. The Catholic theologian Romano Guardini once said that this scene is an analogy for a common experience in the Christian life: spiritual dryness. When we first begin to

grow in our Christian faith as adults, we may feel close to God and experience an enthusiasm for prayer, spiritual reading and sharing the faith with others. However, after some time, this initial sweetness of the Christian life may begin to fade. God no longer seems close to us. Prayer seems dry and pointless. We search for him through all our familiar methods of prayer and devotion, but he is nowhere to be found. Guardini says:

> At first, Christ is the center; our faith in Him is firm and loving. But then He disappears for a while, suddenly and apparently without the slightest reason. A remoteness has been created.... A void is formed. We feel forsaken. Faith seems folly.... Everything becomes heavy, wearisome, and senseless. We must walk alone and seek. But one day we find Christ again—and it is in such circumstances that the power of the Father's will becomes evident to us.[3]

* Describe a time when you felt Jesus was distant, and you could not find him in all the usual places (prayer, fellowship and so forth).

* Why do you think God sometimes *seems* far away from us?

* In moments like this, what can we do to "find Jesus" again?

CHAPTER EIGHT

The Return of the King
Jesus' Family Tree
(Matthew 1:1-17)

The book of the genealogy of Jesus Christ, the son of David, the son of Abraham. Abraham was the father of Isaac, and Isaac the father of Jacob, and Jacob the father of Judah and his brothers, and Judah the father of Perez and Zerah by Tamar, and Perez the father of Hezron, and Hezron the father of Ram, and Ram the father of Amminadab, and Amminadab the father of Nahshon, and Nahshon the father of Salmon, and Salmon the father of Boaz by Rahab, and Boaz the father of Obed by Ruth, and Obed the father of Jesse, and Jesse the father of David the king.

And David was the father of Solomon by the wife of Uriah, and Solomon the father of Rehoboam, and Rehoboam the father of Abijah, and Abijah the father of Asa, and Asa the father of Jehoshaphat, and Jehoshaphat the father of Joram, and Joram the father of Uzziah, and Uzziah the father of Jotham, and Jotham the father of Ahaz, and Ahaz the father of Hezekiah, and Hezekiah the father of Manasseh, and Manasseh the father of Amos, and Amos the father of Josiah, and Josiah the father of Jechoniah and his brothers, at the time of the deportation to Babylon.

And after the deportation to Babylon: Jechoniah was the father of Shealtiel, and Shealtiel the father of Zerubbabel, and Zerubbabel the father of Abiud, and Abiud the father of

Eliakim, and Eliakim the father of Azor, and Azor the father of Zadok, and Zadok the father of Achim, and Achim the father of Eliud, and Eliud the father of Eleazar, and Eleazar the father of Matthan, and Matthan the father of Jacob, and Jacob the father of Joseph the husband of Mary, of whom Jesus was born, who is called Christ.

—MATTHEW 1:1-17

ONE HAS TO WONDER why Matthew begins his Gospel with a long genealogy. If the Gospel is supposed to be "good news," couldn't there be a more captivating way of introducing it? As one New Testament scholar has said, "Let's face it: Other people's family trees are about as interesting as other people's holiday videos."[1] So why did Matthew begin the most important story ever told with what seems to be the dullest of introductions—a list of forty-seven names?

It is true that for most readers today, encountering a biblical genealogy is about as exciting as reading names in a telephone book. However, for first-century Jews the names in Matthew's genealogy would have been the most dramatic news they had received in a long time. In fact, if there were modern media in ancient Palestine, this genealogy would have made the front page of the *New York Times* and served as the lead story on CNN.

What would they have seen in this genealogy that modern readers tend to miss? For the ancient Jews, a genealogy was not simply a list of people who lived hundreds of years before. Rather, each name told a story and recalled important places, events and periods in Israel's history. Matthew strategically compressed that story into seventeen verses to show how God's plan for Israel is reaching its climax in the child mentioned at the end of this family tree.

Back to the Beginning

"The book of the genealogy of Jesus Christ, the son of David, the son of Abraham" (Matthew 1:1).

Matthew does not waste any time hooking us into this Old Testament story. In fact, before he mentions a single name in Jesus' family tree, Matthew's very first words, "The book of the genealogy," bring us all the way back to the beginning of the Bible, the Book of Genesis.

Matthew 1:1 can be translated literally, "*The book of the genesis* of Jesus Christ." This is significant because similar expressions were used in Genesis to announce great beginnings that took place at the dawn of creation. For example, a similar formula was used to sum up the story of how God created the universe: "These are the generations of the heavens and the earth when they were created" (Genesis 2:4). This formula also was used to introduce the family tree of our first parents, Adam and Eve: "the book of the generations of Adam" (Genesis 5:1). In Genesis 10:1 the same phrase introduced the genealogy of Noah's family—the new human family who survived after the flood.

In each of these cases—Adam and creation, Noah and the flood—the phrase "the book of the genealogy" signals a significant starting point in God's plan for humanity. By opening his Gospel with these words, Matthew announces that another new beginning is here. The child at the end of this genealogy will bring about a new genesis: the renewal of all humanity and the restoration of the entire created order into harmony with God.

Worldwide Blessing

Matthew 1:1 goes on to describe Jesus as "the son of Abraham." For an ancient Israelite, such a description means a lot more than being a physical descendant of this great patriarch. Being a son of Abraham is at the very heart of Israelite national identity.

God promised Abraham that his descendants one day would become a great *nation* (see Genesis 12:2; see also 15:18) and that *kings* eventually would come forth from Abraham's line (Genesis 17:6, 16). Jews in the first century would have seen that these two promises already were fulfilled when Israel became a *nation* in the time of Moses and a *kingdom* in the time of David.

However, there was one promise made to Abraham that had yet to be fulfilled, and it was the greatest promise of all. In response to Abraham's faithfulness, God swore that Abraham's descendants eventually would serve as *an instrument to bring blessing to all the peoples of the world*: "And by your descendants shall all the nations of the earth bless themselves, because you have obeyed my voice" (Genesis 22:18). This third promise gave rise to the Jewish belief that, one day, people from all the pagan nations would come to worship the one true God and be reunited with Israel in one covenant family.

By tracing Jesus' lineage specifically to Abraham, Matthew is drawing our attention to this worldwide mission of Israel. And such an allusion might stir hope that the child at the end of the genealogy will be the one to fulfill the long-awaited third promise and bring blessing to the entire human family.

"The Son of David"

While many names are mentioned in the genealogy, David and Solomon stand out together as one of the highest points in this family tree. A first-century Jew reading about "David the king" and his son Solomon certainly would recall the glory days of the kingdom of Israel. These men were the royal heroes of old who brought Israel to its greatest moment in history. In the time of David and Solomon, three important symbols of Israel's national identity—the land, the king and the temple—shined most brightly.

The Land

The Promised Land was more than a place for God's people to dwell. It was like a new Eden, the home for the covenant family of God. It was the place where Yahweh would bestow blessings on his people and where he one day would regather the pagan nations to himself. Israel first entered the Promised Land in the days of Joshua but the nation struggled against foreign invaders for several generations. Through David's military victories, the people of Israel found rest from all their enemies (see 2 Samuel 7:1) and finally were able to dwell securely in the land for the first time in several centuries.

The King

The Davidic kingdom, however, was much more than a political and military entity leading the Israelite people. The kingdom was based on a covenant God made with David's family, and it had a universal scope. God promised David and his descendants aneverlasting dynasty. And the Scriptures foretold that this kingdom would extend to the ends of the earth.

In fact, a glimpse of the kingdom's international influence already can be seen in the time of David and Solomon. At that time foreign nations became servants of Israel, made covenants with Israel and even came to the Israelite king to learn of the wisdom God had given to him (see 2 Samuel 8; 2 Samuel 10:14; 1 Kings 9–10; Psalms 72, 89 and 132).

The Temple

For the ancient Israelites, the temple in Jerusalem was not just a place of worship; it was the center of the universe. The Jews believed that the one true God who created the entire cosmos dwelt in a unique way with the Jewish people in this sacred spot.

God's presence first came to Israel in the form of a cloud in the time of Moses. The glory-cloud of the Lord hovered over the ark of the covenant, which was kept in the portable sanctuary known as the tabernacle or "tent of meeting." When David became king, he brought the ark to the capital city of Jerusalem. There he wanted to build a permanent sanctuary—a magnificent temple—to house the ark and God's presence.

David's son Solomon carried out these plans. He had the ark brought into the innermost chamber of the temple, known as "the Holy of Holies." When Solomon dedicated the temple, God's glory-cloud filled the sanctuary, signifying that the God of the universe dwelt in a special way among the Jews in Jerusalem (see 1 Kings 8:1-13).

All this—Israel's land, the Davidic kingdom and God's presence in the temple—were associated with the two foundational kings mentioned in verse 6, David and Solomon.

The Downfall of Israel

However, the genealogy in Matthew 1 does not stop with David and Solomon. The subsequent verses introduce their many wicked successors, who led the kingdom to its downfall: Rehoboam, Abijah and so forth (see Matthew 1:7-10). The painful memories of these unfaithful Jewish rulers reach their lowest point in verse 11, which says that Josiah was "the father of

Jeconiah and his brothers, *at the time of the deportation to Babylon.*"

This line represents the most somber note in the genealogy, recalling the tragic events of 586 B.C. Matthew does not mention "the time of deportation to Babylon" simply as a chronological marker. Rather, this verse brings to mind all that the Jews lost when Babylon invaded Jerusalem and carried the people away into exile. This was the moment when Israel lost the three great symbols of their national identity: the land, the king and the temple.

First, the exile represented the loss of *the land.* The Jews were driven off the Promised Land and sent to Babylon, where they became slaves among the pagans. Even though they returned in 515 B.C., the Jews never really recovered control of their land. Rather, one foreign nation after another ruled over them. This is why Jewish leaders who were rebuilding Jerusalem in this time period described themselves as being slaves in their own land (see Ezra 9:8-9; Nehemiah 9:36).[2] In Jesus' day the oppressive conditions continued, as the Romans controlled the land that once had been the prized possession of God's people.

Second, the events of 586 B.C. marked the end of the Davidic *kingdom.* When Babylon invaded Jerusalem, the troops targeted the royal family, capturing the king and his sons. Before plucking out the king's eyes and carrying him off into exile, the Babylonians gave him one last sight: that of his own sons being slain before him (see 2 Kings 25:6-7). No son of David ruled on the throne in Jerusalem for the next six centuries, up to the time of Christ. Thus the everlasting dynasty appeared to come to an abrupt halt with Babylon's destruction of Jerusalem.

The Lost Ark

Third, one could argue that the destruction of *the temple* represented the most devastating blow to the Jewish people. Babylon destroyed the temple, desecrating God's holy house and carrying away many of the sacred vessels used for liturgical worship. Israel's most important treasure—the ark of the covenant—was spared when, just before the Babylonians invaded Jerusalem, the prophet Jeremiah brought it out of the temple and hid it in a mountain (see 2 Maccabees 2:4-8). However, God's presence left the temple, and the ark was never found again.

The Jews returned to Jerusalem to rebuild their temple in 515 B.C., yet the new house of God was missing its most revered vessel—the ark of the covenant, which carried God's presence. Although the temple still represented the holiest spot on the face of the earth, the Jews were longing for God's presence to return to Jerusalem and to be with his people again, as it did in the days before the exile.[3]

All this was lost in 586 B.C.—the land, the king and the temple—and Israel was still suffering the consequences at the time of Jesus' birth. A Jew reading about "the deportation to Babylon" in verse 11 could not help but bring this to mind. The Jews still did not have control over their land. They still did not have a son of David to rule them. And they still were longing for God's presence to be with them again in the temple.

The Hope of Zerubbabel

Nevertheless, God offered the Jewish people hope in the midst of their sufferings. Through the prophets he announced that one day he would send a new royal descendant of David, a new anointed king called "the Messiah" (meaning "anointed one"). This Messiah-King would usher in a new era in which the Jews would regain the land, the kingdom would be restored to its former glory, and God's presence would return to Israel (see Ezekiel 43:2-5; 44:4).

Matthew's Gospel calls upon those hopes when it introduces a man named Zerubbabel, who stands as a turning point in the genealogy. As one of the leaders in the rebuilding of Jerusalem in 515 B.C., Zerubbabel represents the last Davidic descendant in Matthew's genealogy for which there is any public record in the Jewish Scriptures. What happened to the sons of David from this period all the way up to the time of Jesus remained somewhat of a mystery, for the Old Testament offered little genealogical record for the royal line of David after Zerubbabel.

This is what would make verses 13-16 so exciting to the original hearers of Matthew's Gospel: The royal line has continued for many generations after Zerubbabel! With each new name—Abiud, Eliakim, Azor and so on—Matthew's genealogy introduces another Davidic descendant previously unknown in the Hebrew Scriptures. The genealogy thus picks up momentum in these verses, building hope that at the end of this family tree we might find that ultimate son of David whom the prophets foretold would return Israel to its former glory.

The Return of the King

Finally the genealogy's rushing crescendo reaches its peak in verse 16, which resounds with the joyful presentation of "Joseph the husband of Mary, of whom Jesus was born, who is called Christ." Here the royal line culminates with the child who will bring Israel's history to its ultimate destination.

The significance of this child can be seen in the three titles he receives in this opening chapter of Matthew's Gospel: Jesus, Christ and Emmanuel. Perhaps one could see in these three names hope that the three Jewish symbols that were shattered in the exile now would be restored: the land, the king and God's presence in the temple.

First, in Hebrew the name *Jesus* itself means "Yahweh saves." And Matthew highlights that the child is given this name for a specific reason: "for he will save his people from their sins" (1:21). This is significant because, according to the Jewish Scriptures, it was Israel's sin that led to their losing the Promised Land. Sin led to the exile. Hence, the deepest problem that Israel faced was not exile from the land but exile from God. Matthew 1:21 underscores the fact that this child Jesus has come primarily to save Israel not from the Roman forces occupying their land but from a much deeper form of oppression: "He will save the people from their sins."

It is also significant that the child's name, "Jesus," is a short-ened form of the name "Joshua." This might recall the famous Old Testament Joshua, Moses' successor who brought the Exodus story to its climax by guiding the people into the Promised Land. Just as the Joshua of old led Israel out of the desert wilderness and into the land, so now Jesus—the new Joshua—will lead the people out of their spiritual exile from God and into the true Promised Land of heaven.

Second, Jesus is given the royal title "Christ" (1:16). In the New Testament the Greek word *christos* commonly translated the Hebrew word *messiah* ("anointed one"). This was the title for the future son of David, whom the prophets said would restore the dynasty and bring to fulfillment the promises about a worldwide, everlasting kingdom. Matthew's genealogy joyfully proclaims that Jesus is that Messiah-King—the first Davidic Son to reign in over five centuries and the one who would restore the kingdom to Israel.

Finally, perhaps the most profound title given to Jesus comes at the end of Matthew's opening chapter. In Matthew 1:23 Jesus is called "Emmanuel," which means "God with us." We cannot overestimate how much this title would have meant for the first-century Jewish people.

Recall how God's visible presence had not dwelt in the temple for more than five hundred years. Without a king, without control of their land and especially without the glory of the Lord dwelling among them, the Jews in the first century might have felt somewhat abandoned. After six centuries of foreign oppression, many would have been wondering what had happened to God's commitment to Israel and all the great promises he had made to their ancestors. They certainly would have been longing for God to be with them again.

In the midst of this uncertainty, Matthew announces that the child at the end of this genealogy is "Emmanuel, which means God with us." In other words, God is with his people again! What is most astonishing, however, is that God is with his people in a way like never before. In ages past, God manifested his presence in the form of a cloud in the temple. Now the God of the universe actually dwells among them in the person of Jesus Christ.

We, too, can delight in this mystery of Emmanuel as God continues to be present to us today. He is present in the Scriptures, in prayer, in the sacraments, and especially in the Eucharist (see *Catechism of the Catholic Church*, #1373). In fact, we can see Christ's desire to be with us until the end of time in his very last words to the apostles in Matthew's Gospel: "Go therefore and make disciples of all nations, baptizing them in the name of the Father and of the Son and of the Holy Spirit, teaching them to observe all that I have commanded you; and lo, I am with you always, to the close of the age (Matthew 28:19–20, emphasis added).

Reflection Questions

1. For most modern readers a biblical genealogy seems like a long, dull list of names. How did ancient Jews view genealogies? Why would they find them so interesting?

2. Why would Matthew begin his Gospel with *this* genealogy?

3. Read Genesis 12:1-3. What promises did God make to Abraham and his descendants in these verses? In light of this background, why do you think Matthew showcases Jesus as "the son of Abraham" in the very first verse of his Gospel?

4. How does Matthew 1:6 represent a high point in this genealogy? Consider the promises God made to David in 2 Samuel 7:10-14.

5. In what way does Matthew 1:11 represent a tragic moment in this genealogy? Consider what happens in 2 Kings 24:10-14; 25:8-9.

6. Who is Zerubbabel (Matthew 1:12)? Why would the names that come after him interest and excite the ancient Jews?

7. What is the meaning of the title *Christ* given to Jesus in 1:16?

8. What does the title *Emmanuel* mean in 1:23?

9. In what ways does Christ remain "with us" today (see
    Matthew 18:20; 28:16-20 and the *Catechism of the Catholic
    Church*, #1374)?

CHAPTER NINE

Silent Knight, Holy Knight
The Annunciation to Joseph
(Matthew 1:18-25)

Now the birth of Jesus Christ took place in this way. When his mother Mary had been betrothed to Joseph, before they came together she was found to be with child of the Holy Spirit; and her husband Joseph, being a just man and unwilling to put her to shame, resolved to send her away quietly. But as he considered this, behold, an angel of the Lord appeared to him in a dream, saying, "Joseph, son of David, do not fear to take Mary your wife, for that which is conceived in her is of the Holy Spirit; she will bear a son, and you shall call his name Jesus, for he will save his people from their sins."

—MATTHEW 1:18-21

W<small>E DO NOT KNOW</small> much about the life of Joseph. In all the New Testament, he has no lines and few dramatic actions. Luke's Gospel simply portrays him as betrothed to Mary, coming from the royal line of David and living in the insignificant village of Nazareth. In Matthew's Gospel Joseph is "the husband of Mary" and the foster father of Jesus, serving as the guardian of the Holy Family. He transports his wife and child from Bethlehem to Egypt in order to avoid Herod's plot to kill the Christ child. Then

Joseph leads his family back to Nazareth when the murderous threat has subsided.

Although we know a little about what Joseph does, we do not know much at all about *who* this man really is on the inside. What Joseph was thinking, hoping or fearing about his wife's extraordinary pregnancy and his own unique calling to serve as the foster father of Israel's Messiah remains, for the most part, a great mystery.

However, in this scene in which the angel appears to Joseph, we catch a glimpse into the soul of this mysterious man. Mary is pregnant, and Joseph decides "to send her away quietly" because he is "a just man" and does not want to put her to shame. What is Joseph planning to do? What does it mean "to send her away quietly"? And why does he want to do it?

Over the centuries there have been diverse answers to these questions. While the precise nature of Joseph's intentions may continue to be as mysterious as the man himself, we will at least consider briefly three common interpretive options for this passage.[1]

Joseph's Dilemma

As explained earlier, betrothal in first-century Judaism was the first stage of a two-step marriage process. As people who were betrothed, Mary and Joseph would have given their legal consent to marry each other and would be considered husband and wife.

The second step involved the consummation of the marriage and the husband's taking his wife to his own home. In this account Mary and Joseph were betrothed but not yet at the second stage of living together. It is within this context that Mary is found to be with child, and Joseph decides to "send her away quietly."

One interpretation of this passage holds that Joseph learns of Mary's pregnancy and assumes that she has committed adultery, since he knows the child is not his. In accordance with Jewish law (see Deuteronomy 24:1-4), Joseph would be expected to seek a divorce. However, the Law also said that a woman who committed adultery should be stoned to death (see Deuteronomy 22:20-21). Since Joseph is "a just man," he in the end decides to divorce her secretly in order to spare Mary the severe punishment of the law. This was the view of church fathers such as Saints John Chrysostom, Ambrose and Augustine.[2]

Others argue that we cannot assume Joseph knew nothing about Mary's conceiving by the Holy Spirit. On a basic human level, it is difficult to imagine that Mary would not tell Joseph about the most amazing event in her life. If an angel appeared to her and told her that she would have a child who would be Israel's long-awaited Messiah-King and that she would conceive of this child as a virgin by the power of God's Holy Spirit, is it likely that she would neglect to mention anything about this to her own husband? Such extreme secrecy seems rather improbable.

Along these lines, a second interpretation holds that Joseph already has knowledge that Mary has conceived by the Holy Spirit. Saints Ephraim, Basil, Bernard and Thomas Aquinas were of this mind-set. Realizing that God is working in Mary's life in a profound way, Joseph responds with religious awe. In humility he feels inadequate to serve as Mary's husband. He desires to release her from the obligation of marriage because of his reverence for the extraordinary work God is doing in her life.[3] It is at this moment that the angel appears to assure Joseph of his vocation to be the head of the Holy Family: "*Do not fear* to take Mary your wife."

A third interpretation held by Saint Jerome views Joseph as simply not knowing what to think about Mary's pregnancy. He knows Mary is with child, and he knows the baby is not his. At the same time he is certain that Mary has remained faithful to him. According to this view, Matthew's Gospel introduces Joseph in this tension between the fact of Mary's carrying a child that is not his own and his conviction of her innocence. Joseph remains in this dilemma until the angel comes to explain where the baby came from: the Holy Spirit.

Emmanuel

> All this took place to fulfill what the Lord had spoken by the prophet:
> "Behold, a virgin shall conceive and bear a son,
> and his name shall be called Emmanuel"
> (which means, God with us). When Joseph woke from sleep, he did as the angel of the Lord commanded him; he took his wife, but knew her not until she had borne a son; and he called his name Jesus.
>
> —MATTHEW 1:22-25

While Joseph's initial response to Mary's pregnancy may continue to be debated, one point that is clear from this passage is that Matthew's Gospel sees Jesus' birth from a virgin as the ultimate fulfillment of the Emmanuel prophecy in Isaiah 7:14. This oracle, which Matthew quotes for us in verse 23, comes from the prophet Isaiah during a crisis in the kingdom of Judah in the eighth century B.C. Foreign armies threatened to invade Jerusalem and destroy the kingdom, while the Jewish king, Ahaz, feared that the Davidic dynasty might be coming to an end and that he would be the last of its kings (Isaiah 7:1-12).

Isaiah's prophecy, however, offered hope for the kingdom in these dark times. It foretold that a young woman of marriageable age (who in ancient Israelite culture would generally be a virgin)[4] would give birth to a royal son, who would continue the Davidic dynasty and who would live to see the retreat of the foreign nations that were threatening Jerusalem (see Isaiah 7:13-17). This child was to be called "Emmanuel," which means "God with us," to underscore how God was still with the Davidic kingdom in this time of trial, just as he had been with the dynasty's founder, King David (see 2 Samuel 7:9).

This prophecy found an initial fulfillment in the son of Ahaz, King Hezekiah. As a royal son, Hezekiah represented the continuation of the Davidic dynasty. He also was the king who witnessed the end of the threat to Jerusalem that his father had faced (see 2 Kings 19), showing that God was still with the kingdom of Judah.

Although the prophecy received its first fulfillment in King Hezekiah, Jews continued to find hope in this passage for a future fulfillment—for an even greater royal son still yet to come. Despite the fact that Hezekiah was a king who "did what was right in the eyes of the Lord" (2 Kings 18:3) and witnessed the dynasty's survival through crisis, his reforms did not last, and the kingdom of Judah eventually was destroyed by another invading force, Babylon. Jews then would have seen more clearly how this prophecy about a child, born of a virgin[5] and coming from the house of David, was associated with God's larger plan, as foretold by Isaiah, to send a new anointed son of David to establish an everlasting dynasty that would reign over all the nations (see Isaiah 9; 11; 2 Samuel 7:8-17).

It is to this secondary fulfillment that Matthew is drawing our attention. Matthew clearly views Jesus, the new royal son of

David, born of the virgin Mary, as the ultimate fulfillment of this prophecy from Isaiah. He will be the one to restore the kingdom and bring Israel's history to its climax. God will be with him as he promised to be with the house of David. Hence he shall be called Emmanuel, "God with us."

Did Joseph Know His Wife?

One brief note on Matthew 1:25: Catholic readers sometimes are puzzled when they come across this verse stating that Joseph took Mary as his wife but "knew her not *until* she had borne a son." In the Bible "to know" one's wife is to know her covenantally—in other words, to have sexual relations with her. At first glance this verse may seem to imply that while Joseph did not have marital relations with Mary *before* Jesus was born, *after* Christ's birth he did. This seems to run counter to the Catholic teaching that Mary remained a virgin throughout her life (see *Catechism of the Catholic Church*, #499-500).

However, the Greek word *heos*, which is translated "until," is used much differently from the way we use the word *until* today. For example, when someone says in English, "Bob was working *until* 4 P.M.," it implies that after 4 P.M. Bob stopped working. Not so in the Greek. If someone says in Greek, "Bob was working until (*heos*) 4 P.M.," this would tell us only that Bob worked up to the point of 4 P.M. It implies nothing about what Bob did afterward.

One example from the Greek translation of the Old Testament that was commonly used in Jesus' day can make this point clear. Consider 2 Samuel 6:23: "And Michal the daughter of Saul had no child to (*heos*) the day of her death." Could this possibly mean that she started having children after she died? Of course not! The Greek word *heos* only tells us about a time period up to a certain point, without in any way implying a change after that point.

Hence, when Matthew 1:25 says that Joseph "knew her not *until* (*heos*) she had borne a son," this does not tell us anything about what happened between Mary and Joseph *after* Jesus was born. It only tells us that they did not have marital relations up to the time of Jesus' birth.

Old Joseph, New Joseph

Before we leave this scene, let us consider one of the most interesting details about the way Joseph appears in Matthew's Gospel. In the opening chapters of the first Gospel, Joseph seems to replay the life of another famous Joseph in the Bible, Joseph the patriarch from the Book of Genesis.

To appreciate the parallels between these two heroic men, let us first briefly recall the story of the Old Testament Joseph. This Joseph of old was the eleventh of Jacob's twelve sons, but he was his father's favorite because he was the son of his father's old age (see Genesis 37:3). This made Joseph the least favorite among his older brothers. They were envious of him for being "daddy's favorite."

Although Joseph's older brothers treated him unfairly, he naively did not do much to help the situation. By sharing with his brothers some of his strange dreams, Joseph only made them all the more infuriated. For example, he once told them about a dream that symbolized that his brothers one day would bow down before him: "Hear this dream which I have dreamed: behold, we were binding sheaves in the field, and lo, my sheaf arose and stood upright; and behold, your sheaves gathered round it, and bowed down to my sheaf" (Genesis 37:6-7).

This probably was not the best way for Joseph to "win friends and influence people"! His brothers responded angrily, "Are you indeed to reign over us? Or are you indeed to have dominion over us?" (37:8).

On a second occasion Joseph told his brothers of another vision he had: "Behold, I have dreamed another dream; and behold, the sun, the moon, and eleven stars were bowing down to me" (37:9). Here the sun and moon represented Joseph's parents, and the eleven stars symbolized his brothers. This dream only angered his brothers further. Even Joseph's father was in disbelief over Joseph's dream: "Shall I and your mother and your brothers indeed come to bow ourselves to the ground before you?" (37:10).

One day Joseph came out to the fields to meet his brothers. They grabbed him and threw him into a cistern, then sold him into slavery. They told their father that Joseph had been killed by a wild animal. Joseph ended up a slave in Egypt, working for a man named Potiphar (see 37:12-36). While Joseph served his master faithfully, Potiphar's wife attempted day after day to seduce him. Joseph remained a loyal servant to his master and a chaste man of God, consistently refusing her.

Eventually, after Joseph repeatedly denied Potiphar's wife, she falsely accused Joseph of trying to seduce *her*. Being framed in this way and unable to defend himself, Joseph was immediately thrown into prison (see chapter 39).

The Impossible Dream?

While in the Egyptian prison, Joseph became well-known for interpreting the dreams of his fellow prisoners and revealing the future through those dreams (see chapter 40). Joseph was such a famous dream interpreter that when Pharaoh had strange visions at night about seven fat cows and seven thin cows, he called upon Joseph to interpret his dream. Joseph told Pharaoh that the seven fat cows represented seven years of great harvest that would be coming in the land, and the seven skinny cows represented seven years of great famine that would follow. Joseph then advised Pharaoh to use the seven years of plenty to stock up on food. This way, when the years of famine hit the land of Egypt, he would be able to feed the people.

Pharaoh not only appreciated Joseph's dream interpretation but also his political counsel—so much so that he rewarded him with the second most powerful position in the kingdom: "You shall be over my house, and all my people shall order themselves as you command; only as regards the throne will I be greater than you" (41:40). As a result, Joseph found himself suddenly released from the Egyptian prison and placed at the top of Pharaoh's government. During the years of famine, Joseph was in charge of distributing the grain to all the people who came to Egypt looking for food (see 41:53-57).

Eventually Joseph's brothers traveled to Egypt in search of grain, and ironically they had to go through Pharaoh's second-in-command, who happened to be their brother Joseph. As a result, Joseph's dreams about his unexpected authority over his family were fulfilled (see 42–45; 50:18). Joseph ended up reunited with his father and his brothers, and he saved his family from the famine by having them dwell with him in Egypt.

Mary's "Most Chaste Spouse"

In many ways Joseph's life can be seen as a prefiguring of the New Testament Joseph, the husband of Mary. Let us consider the numerous parallels between these two great men.

First, they not only are both called Joseph, but even their fathers share a common name, Jacob (see Genesis 37:2-3; Matthew 1:16). Second, both are persecuted. Joseph's brothers sell him into slavery, and King Herod tries to kill Joseph's adopted son, Jesus. Third, both end up in Egypt as a result of their persecution. Joseph of old becomes a slave in Egypt, while the New Testament Joseph travels there in order to flee from Herod's terror.

Fourth, both Josephs are famous for their dreams. We have seen how Joseph the patriarch is well-known for his dreams and for interpreting other people's dreams. Meanwhile, Joseph in Matthew's Gospel stands out for his own unusual dreams. An angel appears to him in a dream in order to tell him to take Mary as his wife and to name the child Jesus (see Matthew 1:20-23). An angel in a second dream warns him of Herod's plot to kill the child and tells him to flee to Egypt (2:13). Again in a third dream, an angel tells him that it is safe to return to the land of Israel (2:19-20). And on the way back Joseph is warned in yet another dream to avoid the land of Judea and travel back to Galilee (2:22). It seems that every scene with Joseph involves an angel of the Lord appearing to him in a dream and telling him to do something or go somewhere. At least in the narrative of Matthew's Gospel, poor Joseph does not seem to get much sleep!

Fifth, both Josephs are well-known for their purity. In the Jewish tradition the most famous virtue of Joseph the patriarch was his chastity, stemming from his steadfast purity while facing the temptation of Potiphar's wife.[6] Similarly, Christian tradition has held up Joseph the husband of Mary as a model for purity. After all, Joseph did not "know" his wife during her pregnancy (see 1:25), and, according to Catholic tradition, Mary and Joseph remained celibate throughout the entirety of their marriage. Fittingly, Joseph has often been called Mary's "most chaste spouse."

Unusual Authority

Sixth, both Josephs find themselves heads over those they naturally should not have authority over. As a younger brother, Joseph of old would be expected to show honor to his father and to his older siblings. However, as the second-in-command in Egypt and as the distributor of the grains to the rest of the world, Joseph surprisingly ends up in a position of authority over his own father and his older brothers, who even bow at his feet (see Genesis 50:18).

Similarly, the New Testament Joseph becomes the head of the Holy Family, serving as the husband of the virgin Mary and as father of the Messiah-King, who is the Son of God. Especially from a Catholic perspective, Joseph's role of authority in the Holy Family would be very intimidating. Put yourself in his shoes. On one hand, he is called to lead a wife who is without sin, never does anything wrong and is the holiest woman of all time. On the other hand, he is called to raise a child who not only *thought* he was God but *really was* God!

Finally, both Josephs are known for their role as the protector and rescuer of their families. Joseph of old ends up saving his family from starvation, while Joseph of the New Testament protects his family from the murderous plot of Herod. This is why

Saint Joseph is considered the patron saint of the Catholic Church as a whole. Just as Joseph protected the Holy Family in the first century, he continues through his intercession to protect the holy family of God today, the Church. In the words of Pope Leo XIII,

> Joseph was in his day the lawful and natural guardian, head and defender of the Holy Family.... It is thus fitting and most worthy of Joseph's dignity that, in the same way that he once kept unceasing holy watch over the family of Nazareth, so now does he protect and defend with his heavenly patronage the Church of Christ.[7]

Reflection Questions

1. Why did Joseph want to send Mary away quietly in Matthew 1:19? Discuss Joseph's possible motives in this scene. Which do you find most plausible? Which do you find most inspiring?

2. Read Matthew 1:24. Compare Joseph's response to the angel's message and Mary's response to the angel's message in Luke 1:38. What does this tell us about the moral character of Jesus' human parents?

3. What do the following verses tell us about Joseph's trust in God and obedience to the Lord's commands in regard to his responsibility of leading the Holy Family?

   * Matthew 1:24

   * Matthew 2:13-14

* Matthew 2:19-21

* Matthew 2:22

4. Explain Matthew 1:25. Does this imply that Joseph had sexual relations with Mary sometime after Jesus was born? Explain. See also *Catechism of the Catholic Church*, #500-507. According to the *Catechism*, what are some of the reasons Mary remained a virgin through her life?

5. In what ways does the Old Testament patriarch Joseph prefigure the New Testament Joseph?

6. The Catholic Church honors the Holy Family as the model family. In what ways does Joseph model Christian fatherhood? What characteristics about Joseph do you think are especially crucial for fathers today?

CHAPTER TEN

The Terror of Herod
The Magi and the Flight to Egypt
(Matthew 2:1-23)

Now when Jesus was born in Bethlehem of Judea in the days of Herod the king, behold, wise men from the East came to Jerusalem, saying, "Where is he who has been born king of the Jews? For we have seen his star in the East, and have come to worship him." When Herod the king heard this, he was troubled, and all Jerusalem with him; and assembling all the chief priests and scribes of the people, he inquired of them where the Christ was to be born. They told him, "In Bethlehem of Judea; for so it is written by the prophet:

'And you, O Bethlehem, in the land of Judah,
are by no means least among the rulers of Judah;
for from you shall come a ruler
who will govern my people Israel.'"

Then Herod summoned the wise men secretly and ascertained from them what time the star appeared; and he sent them to Bethlehem, saying, "Go and search diligently for the child, and when you have found him bring me word, that I too may come and worship him." When they had heard the king they went their way; and lo, the star which they had seen in the East went before them, till it came to rest over the place where the child was. When they saw the star, they rejoiced exceedingly with great joy; and going into the house they saw the child with Mary his mother, and they fell down and worshiped him. Then, opening their treasures, they offered him gifts, gold and frankincense and myrrh. And being warned in a dream not to return to Herod, they departed to their own country by another way.

—MATTHEW 2:1-12

"READING MATTHEW, ONE GETS the feeling the author put together his gospel with the precision of a Swiss watch."[1] So said one New Testament scholar when describing the highly systematic approach Matthew takes in narrating the coming of the Messiah.

Addressing an audience with a strong Jewish background, Matthew, perhaps more than any other evangelist, highlights that Jesus is the one who fulfills all the old covenant hopes and prophecies. Practically every line in his Gospel is charged with allusions to the Old Testament.

Such precision is what we should expect from a man like Matthew. As a former tax collector, he would be trained in scribal skills and detailed note-taking. Attention to detail would have been his specialty. Matthew especially would have paid close attention to the details of Christ's life and how those details fit into God's larger plan of salvation. Thus it is not surprising that Matthew's Gospel constantly points the reader to one Old Testament passage after another throughout his narrative.

There are two ways that Matthew's Gospel highlights Christ's fulfilling Old Testament prophecies and expectations. One approach makes clear, explicit connections to Old Testament passages, while the other approach involves more subtle allusions to the Jewish Scriptures.

"Prophecy for Dummies"

Matthew often uses explicit formula statements in order to highlight for the reader that a prophecy is being fulfilled. In these cases he tells a story from the life of Jesus and then says something along the lines of "This was done to fulfill what was spoken by the prophet...." This "fulfillment formula" then introduces a quote from an Old Testament prophecy that Matthew believes has come to fulfillment in Christ.

We already have seen one instance of this approach to biblical prophecy in Matthew 1. There we read that the virgin Mary conceived a child by the Holy Spirit (see 1:18). Matthew then proceeds to make it very clear that this virginal conception fulfills the Emmanuel prophecy of Isaiah 7:14. First he uses a typical formula statement, "All this took place to fulfill what the Lord had spoken by the prophet...." Then he quotes the actual prophecy for us so that we can see the fulfillment clearly (see 1:22-23).

One might think of this method as the "Biblical Prophecy for Dummies" approach. One does not need to know a lot about the Old Testament to realize that a prophecy is coming to fulfillment. Matthew connects the dots for us, first by explicitly alerting us to the fact that prophecy has been fulfilled and then by quoting for us the actual Old Testament passage that he believes is coming to fruition.

Another example of this approach comes in Matthew 2. After Herod hears of the Magi's coming to Jerusalem in search of a newborn king, he asks the chief priests and scribes where the Messiah is expected to be born. They respond:

> In Bethlehem of Judea; *for so it is written by the prophet*:
> "And you, O Bethlehem, in the land of Judah,

are by no means least among the rulers of Judah;
for from you shall come a ruler
who will govern my people Israel."

—MATTHEW 2:5-6, emphasis added

Here again Matthew announces prophetic fulfillment with the typical formulaic statement and then provides a quotation from the prophecy he has in mind. In this case he quotes a part of Micah 5:1-4, which announced that a new shepherd-like Davidic king would come to restore Israel and extend his reign to the ends of the earth. And Micah foretold that this great king would be born in the same city where David was born: Bethlehem.

Whose Line Is It Anyway?

Matthew does not always make things that easy. Since he is writing to an audience with a strong Jewish background, he assumes that his readers know the Old Testament stories like the backs of their hands. Consequently, he often simply alludes to the Jewish Scriptures without explicitly citing every passage he has in mind.

In fact, one might say that Matthew assumes his readers know the Old Testament stories the way many Americans know the lines from popular songs, movies and commercials. Hearing someone mention "the golden arches" brings to mind a popular fast food restaurant. Mention of a "light saber" may cause us to envision Jedi Knights battling the dark powers with these glowing, swordlike weapons. And if we were to hear someone merely say "Hey, Jude," many of us would suddenly have the melody of this famous Beatles song in our heads.

But what happens when someone is not familiar with the culture in which these lines originate? Take, for example, the words, "Oh, say, can you see by the dawn's early light?" For the average American, these words bring to mind patriotism, our national flag and our national identity. However, someone unfamiliar with American culture may not appreciate what these first words of our national anthem express. Someone from another country may even think these words are about someone's eyesight in the early morning hours!

Similarly, when Matthew mentions just a line or a key phrase from an Old Testament prophecy or story, he is alluding to a larger story and bringing to mind a wider cultural context. And he assumes that we are following his allusions. However, if we are not familiar with the Old Testament background, we may miss the very message Matthew is trying to communicate. The more we get in tune with the Old Testament, the more we will hear the beautiful harmonies of salvation history being brought to a crescendo in Matthew's Gospel.

Three Men and a Baby?

The scene in which the Magi come looking for the newborn king offers several examples of the array of subtle allusions to the Old Testament that Matthew assumes we will notice.

First, consider the simple line in Matthew 2:4 that tells of Herod's "*assembling* all the chief priests and scribes of the people" (emphasis added). At first glance this statement may not appear to be of great significance. However, for the first-century Jewish readers of this Gospel, these words would bring to mind the famous messianic passage in Psalm 2. This psalm foretold that the powers of this world would assemble together to plot against the Lord's anointed—the Messiah: "The kings of the earth set themselves and the rulers take counsel together, against the Lord and his anointed" (Psalm 2:2). Matthew uses this same language to show Herod, the chief priests and the scribes aligning themselves against the Christ child. Matthew's use of this imagery highlights the fact that at the very beginning of Christ's life, the world's leaders already are plotting against him—just as Psalm 2 foretold.

Moreover, this same language is used later in Matthew's Gospel to describe the chief priests, the elders and the Pharisees who "assembled" and "took counsel" as they were plotting to put Jesus to his death (see Matthew 22:15; 26:3; 27:1). Thus, Christ's persecution in his infancy also serves as a foreshadowing of the attacks he will face as an adult at the height of his public ministry.

A second allusion to the Old Testament is in the story of the Magi as a whole. For many first-century Jewish readers, this plot would sound all too familiar. It would recall the Old Testament story of Balak, Balaam and the prophecy of Numbers 24.

Balak was the king of Moab who feared the Israelites so much that he called upon a pagan prophet from the east named Balaam to put a curse on them. However, whenever Balaam tried to curse Israel, words of blessing mysteriously came out of his mouth.

Three times Balaam attempted to cast a spell on the Israelites, but each time God intervened to cause him to utter blessings (see Numbers 22–24). Even more remarkable is the fact that after his last attempt to curse them, the Spirit of God came upon Balaam, and he spoke in prophecy:

> I see him, but not now;
> I behold him, but not nigh:
> a *star* shall come forth out of Jacob
> and a *scepter* shall rise out of Israel;
> it shall crush the forehead of Moab,
> and break down all the sons of Sheth.

> *Edom* shall be dispossessed...
> while Israel does valiantly.
> —NUMBERS 24:17-18, emphasis added

These prophetic words told of a great leader who would come in the future. The image of a *scepter*, or royal staff, indicated that this person would be a king. The fact that the royal staff "shall rise out of *Israel*" told the people that this great king would be born in the land of the Jews. Furthermore, the prophecy foretold that this king's coming would be accompanied by a *star* that would rise out of the land of Israel ("out of Jacob").[3] When this king arrived, he would defeat Israel's enemies, including *Edom*, who would be dispossessed.

All this prefigures the story of Herod, the Magi and the star in Matthew 2. Just as the wicked King Balak wanted to use a pagan from the East to destroy Israel, so the wicked King Herod tries to use the Magi from the East in his plot to kill Israel's new-born Messiah. Similarly, Balaam prefigures the Magi. Just as Balaam did not cooperate with Balak's plan to harm Israel but ended up blessing God's people, so do the Magi refuse to cooperate with Herod and instead end up paying homage to Jesus and bringing him gifts fit for a king.

Furthermore, the star that the Magi follow in Matthew 2 recalls Balaam's prophecy about a great star over Israel that would signal the coming of a new king of the Jews. One significant point from this prophecy is that it explicitly mentions that when this new king arrives, Israel's enemies will be defeated and even "*Edom* shall be dispossessed." This is interesting because the current king over Israel, King Herod, is not a Jewish king. He is a pagan from *Edom* who was appointed to rule over the land for the Romans. Therefore, the echoes of Balaam's prophecy in

Matthew 2 make one thing clear to the ancient Jewish reader. The days of Herod the Edomite are numbered. "Edom shall be dispossesed." A new King is born in Bethlehem.

Gold, Frankincense and Myrrh

We can see a third example of Matthew's alluding to the Old Testament when the Magi arrive at the house where Jesus is staying. They fall down, worship him and give him gifts of gold, frankincense and myrrh (see Matthew 2:11). For an ancient Jew, this event from the very beginning of Christ's life signals that this child in Bethlehem already is fulfilling his role as the great Davidic king who was expected to come and extend God's kingdom to all the nations.

In this scene Jesus fulfills Psalm 72, which describes how the son of David will have dominion over all the earth and how kings of all nations shall bow down before him and serve him, bringing him gifts of gold (see Psalm 72:10-15). He also fulfills Isaiah 60: "*Nations shall come to your light*, and kings to the brightness of your rising.... They shall bring *gold and frankincense*, and shall proclaim the praise of the Lord" (Isaiah 60:3, 6, emphasis added).

This background clues us in to the fact that as soon as Christ begins his life on earth, he already is drawing all nations together again, just as the prophets foretold. The Magi represent the first of many Gentiles scattered throughout the world who are gathered back into God's covenant family through Christ's saving mission. As the *Catechism of the Catholic Church* explains:

> In the magi, representatives of the neighboring pagan religions, the Gospel sees the first-fruits of the nations, who welcome the good news of salvation through the Incarnation. The

> magi's coming to Jerusalem in order to pay homage to the king
> of the Jews shows that they seek in Israel, in the messianic light
> of the star of David, the one who will be king of the nations.
> (#528)

One last point about the Magi's three gifts is worth mentioning here. Christian tradition has viewed these three gifts as symbolizing three aspects of the mystery of Jesus Christ. Gold represents a gift fit for a king, and thus points to Christ's kingship. Frankincense is a type of incense used in worshipping God, and thus points to Christ's divinity. Myrrh was a burial ointment, and thus points to Christ's humanity, and in particular, it foreshadows his death on the cross.[3]

Out of Egypt

> Now when they had departed, behold, an angel of the Lord
> appeared to Joseph in a dream and said, "Rise, take the child
> and his mother, and flee to Egypt, and remain there till I tell
> you; for Herod is about to search for the child, to destroy him."
> And he rose and took the child and his mother by night, and
> departed to Egypt, and remained there until the death of
> Herod. This was to fulfill what the Lord had spoken by the
> prophet, "Out of Egypt have I called my son."
> —MATTHEW 2:13-15

Here we encounter another one of Matthew's "fulfillment formulas." This time he quotes a passage from Hosea 11:1: "Out of Egypt I called my son." On one hand, this line recalls the Book of Exodus's depiction of Israel's filial-like relationship with God and of God's rescue of his "first-born son" Israel from slavery in Egypt (see Exodus 4:22-23). On the other hand, in the larger context of the Book of Hosea, the prophet employed this Exodus imagery to describe the salvific work God would do for Israel in the *future*—freeing the nation from its enemies once again (see Hosea 2:14-23).

By applying this Exodus motif to the Christ child, Matthew shows that Jesus now embodies Israel's sonship relationship with God. As the representative of Israel, Jesus will relive the Exodus story in his own life. Just as God's people were called out of Egypt and brought to the Promised Land in order to evangelize the nations, soon Jesus will be called out of Egypt to bring Israel's worldwide mission to completion and extend God's salvation to all the earth.

Rachel Weeps

> Then Herod, when he saw that he had been tricked by the wise men, was in a furious rage, and he sent and killed all the male children in Bethlehem and in all that region who were two years old or under, according to the time which he had ascertained from the wise men. Then was fulfilled what was spoken by the prophet Jeremiah:
> "A voice was heard in Ramah,
> wailing and loud lamentation,
> Rachel weeping for her children;
> she refused to be consoled,
> because they were no more."
>
> —Matthew 2:16-18

"In a furious rage," Herod kills all the male children under the age of two in the region around Bethlehem. This picture of Herod fits what we know about him historically. He was violently insecure about his position, murdering any suspected rival and even killing three of his own sons and his favored wife. Matthew places the horror of this latest Herodian atrocity in the context of Old Testament prophecy. Using another fulfillment formula, he draws our attention to Jeremiah 31:15, a somber verse that speaks of

Rachel weeping for her children in the town of Ramah.

Ramah was a city of sorrow in the Old Testament. In the eighth century B.C. the Assyrians attacked it, and in the sixth century B.C. the Babylonians established Ramah as the assembly point for leading the Jewish captives away on the road to exile (see Jeremiah 40:1). This is why Jeremiah spoke of Rachel's weeping for her children and her loud lamentations being heard in Ramah. In Jeremiah 31:15 Rachel, the wife of the patriarch Jacob (and in a sense, the matriarch of all of Israel), is portrayed as weeping bitterly in her grave for her descendants who are being killed and sent off into slavery during the Babylonian invasion.

In light of Herod's massacre, Matthew views Bethlehem as a new city of great suffering, a new Ramah. And he fittingly brings to mind the Jewish tradition of Rachel's weeping for her children, for now it is as if she is weeping once again for the holy innocents who are killed by Herod in Bethlehem.

The Nazareth Prophecy

> But when Herod died, behold, an angel of the Lord appeared in a dream to Joseph in Egypt, saying, "Rise, take the child and his mother, and go to the land of Israel, for those who sought the child's life are dead." And he rose and took the child and his mother, and went to the land of Israel. But when he heard that Archelaus reigned over Judea in place of his father Herod, he was afraid to go there, and being warned in a dream he withdrew to the district of Galilee. And he went and dwelt in a city called Nazareth, that what was spoken by the prophets might be fulfilled, "He shall be called a Nazarene."
>
> —MATTHEW 2:19-23

At the end of Matthew's infancy narrative, he leaves us with one last fulfillment formula. He tells us that Jesus is raised in the city of Nazareth, so that "what was spoken by the prophets might be fulfilled, 'He shall be called a Nazarene.'"

However, there is one major problem with Matthew's assertion about this prophecy fulfillment: There is no single text in the entire Old Testament that says the Messiah would be a Nazarene! Is Matthew just making up a prophecy?

To appreciate what Matthew is doing here, we must first note that he is making a play on words, drawing on the similarities between the word *Nazareth* and the word *neser*, which in Hebrew means "branch." This is significant because the word *branch* was used in the Old Testament to describe the Messiah. For example, Isaiah 11:1 says, "There shall come forth a shoot from the stump of Jesse, and a branch shall grow out of his roots."

What does this symbolize? As the father of King David, Jesse represents the foundation of the Davidic dynasty. Since David's dynasty was depicted as a large tree, its being cut down and reduced to a stump brings to mind the events of 586 B.C., when the Babylonians destroyed the kingdom, took away the king and slaughtered many of his sons. Hence the image of "the stump of Jesse" symbolizes the Davidic dynasty as it appeared to come to an end after the Babylonian invasion.

However, Isaiah 11 offers good news for Jews after 586 B.C. Out of the stump of Jesse a *branch* shall grow. In other words, despite the destruction of Jerusalem, the Davidic line will continue, like a branch rising out of a stump. At the end of this branch shall blossom the Messiah. Isaiah says that one day, someone anointed with the Spirit will come from this branch: "The Spirit of the Lord shall rest upon him." And he will bring about a worldwide kingdom: "The earth shall be full of the knowledge of the LORD as the waters cover the sea. In that day the root of Jesse shall stand as an ensign to the peoples; him shall the nations seek, and his dwellings shall be glorious" (Isaiah 11:9-10).

Other prophets borrowed this image of the branch from Isaiah 11 to describe the future Messiah-King who would restore Israel. For example, Jeremiah 23:5-6 says, "Behold, the days are coming, says the LORD, when I will raise up for David a righteous Branch, and he shall reign as king and deal wisely.... In his days Judah will be saved." In this prophetic passage and others like it, *branch* becomes a symbolic word for the Messiah who will restore the kingdom (see Jeremiah 33:14-16; Zechariah 3:8; 6:11-13).

Thus, while there is no single prophecy that says, "He shall be called a Nazarene," there is a tradition in the Old Testament prophets of describing the Messiah as a "branch" or "shoot." Since Nazareth might bring to mind *branch* (*neser*), Matthew highlights how fitting it is that Jesus—the messianic "branch" whom the prophets foretold—would be raised in the "branch-town" of Nazareth.[4]

A New Moses

We will conclude by considering how Matthew 2 presents Jesus as the new Moses. This is a fitting paradigm for Jesus, since Moses stands out in Israel's history as the savior figure *par excellence*.

Let us briefly recall some key moments in the life of Moses. He was born during Pharaoh's wicked decree to kill all the Hebrew male children in Egypt, but he survived this holocaust when his mother put him in a basket in the Nile River. Pharaoh's daughter discovered Moses there and wanted to raise the child. Moses ironically ended up being saved from the murderous decree by being raised in Pharaoh's own household in Egypt.

When Moses was older, he killed an Egyptian soldier who was treating the Hebrews harshly. As a result, Pharaoh wanted to have him killed, so Moses fled to the wilderness. After forty years God appeared to Moses in the burning bush and told him it was safe to return to Egypt, "for all the men who were seeking your life are dead" (Exodus 4:19).

Moses led the people to freedom across the waters of the Red Sea (see Exodus 14), then he guided them for forty years in the wilderness on their way to the Promised Land. One of the high points along the way came when Moses went up Mount Sinai to receive God's law for the people. God wrote these instructions on tablets of stone, and they became known as the Ten Commandments (see Exodus 20–24).

In many ways Jesus relives the experience of Moses. Like Moses, Jesus also is born during a king's wicked decree to kill the Jewish male children. This time the tyrant's name is Herod, and he orders the death of all the baby boys in the region surrounding Bethlehem who are two years old or younger. Like Moses, Jesus escapes Herod's murderous plot by fleeing to Egypt. Like Moses, Jesus' father is told by the angel that it is now safe for Jesus to return to the land of Israel, "for those who sought the child's life are dead" (Matthew 2:20).

Just as Moses led the people through the waters of the Red Sea and into the wilderness, where they wandered for forty years, so Jesus begins his public ministry by going through the waters of the Jordan River at his baptism (see Matthew 3) and then traveling in the desert for forty days of prayer and fasting (see Matthew 4). One of the high points of Jesus' ministry is when he goes up a mountain to give a new law, the famous Sermon on the Mount (see Matthew 5–7). This is reminiscent of Moses' giving the Ten Commandments to the people at Mount Sinai.

All these parallels do not simply demonstrate that there is some vague, coincidental similarity between Moses and Jesus. For Matthew and the early Christians, the providential hand of God had written these profound connections between the two men into the fabric of the world's history. God gave Israel its first savior figure of Moses not only to rescue the people from slavery in Egypt but also to prefigure and anticipate the new messianic Savior he would send to redeem the whole world. Matthew's Gospel thus highlights the fact that from the very beginning of Christ's life, Moses and the Exodus story serve as an interpretive key for understanding the mission of the Messiah.

Reflection Questions

1. What are the two ways in which Matthew shows Old Testament hopes and prophecies coming to fulfillment in Christ? How can familiarity with the Old Testament deepen your understanding of who Christ is?

2. Why do the Magi look for a king in Israel just because they see a certain star in the sky? See Matthew 2:2 and the prophecy from Numbers 24:15-17.

3. In what specific ways does the story of Balak and Balaam in Numbers 22–24 prefigure the narrative of Herod and the Magi?

4. How do these stories show us that God is truly in charge of the world and all its affairs? How can you embrace this truth of God's providence more fully in your own life?

5. Read Matthew 2:23. What does the word *Nazareth* mean?

6. How does the prophecy in Isaiah 11 relate to this prophecy fulfillment in Matthew 2:23?
    * Read Isaiah 11:1. Who is Jesse? What does the stump symbolize? What does the branch coming out of the stump of Jesse represent?

    * Read Isaiah 11:2. What will this branch have?

    * Read Isaiah 11:6, 9-11. What will God do for Israel and the whole world when the branch of Jesse comes?

7. In what ways does Moses prefigure Jesus in his childhood (see Matthew 2) and throughout his public ministry (in the rest of the Gospel)?

8. The Introduction to this book states: "The goal of this book is to help bring the reader back into the first-century Jewish world so as to discover many of the spiritual treasures that are packed into practically every line and every detail of these Gospel accounts." Has this study helped you see and experience the richness of Scripture and the mystery of Christ's coming? If so, name some specific ways.

Notes

Introduction: "The Hopes and Fears of All the Years"

1. *Sacramentary Supplement* (New York: Catholic Book Publishing, 1994), p. 22.

Chapter One: A New Era Dawning

1. N. Wright, *The New Testament and the People of God* (Minneapolis: Fortress Press, 1992), pp. 378-379.

2. Raymond Brown, *Birth of the Messiah* (Garden City, N.J.: Doubleday, 1977), p. 271.

Chapter Two: The Mother of the King

1. See John Paul II, General Audience of May 8, 1996, in John Paul II, *Theotokos: Woman, Mother, Disciple* (Boston: Pauline, 2000), p. 88. Also John Paul II, *Redemptoris Mater* (RM), 8.

2. John Nolland, *Luke 1-9:20* (Dallas: Word Books, 1989), p. 50; J. Green, *The Gospel of Luke* (Ann Arbor, Mich.: Eerdmans, 1997), p. 87.

3. J. Paredes, *Mary and the Kingdom of God* (Middlegreen, UK: St. Paul, 1991), pp. 69-70.

4. Saint Ignatius of Antioch, *Ad Smyrn.* 1-2 in Joseph B. Lightfoot, ed., *The Apostolic Fathers* (London: Macmillan, 1889), II/2, pp. 289-293. As cited in *CCC*, #496.

5. Ignace De La Potterie, *Mary in the Mystery of the Covenant* (New York: Alba House, 1992), pp. 34-35.

6. For example, see the ecumenical study by Raymond Brown, et. al., *Mary in the New Testament* (Philadelphia: Fortress, 1978), pp. 125-126, 135-37.

Chapter Three: Blessed Among Women

1. Some may also see the angels' praising God in response to the birth of Jesus in Bethlehem in Luke 2:13-14 as the parallel to Zechariah's hymnlike praise of God in response to John's birth.

2. J. Green, *The Gospel of Luke* (Ann Arbor: Eerdmans, 1997), p. 94.

3. Green, p. 96.

4. For more on the biblical queen-mother theme, see E. Sri, *Queen Mother: A Biblical Theology of Mary's Queenship* (Steubenville, Oh.: Emmaus Road, 2005).

5. For a discussion of some of these parallels, see Nolland, pp. 74-77.

6. Nolland, p. 54.

7. See 1 Chronicles 15:25-28; 16:4-5; and 2 Chronicles 5:13 where *anaphanein* is found in the Greek Old Testament. See also, L. Deiss, *Mary, Daughter of Zion* (Collegeville, Minn.: Liturgical Press, 1972), pp. 92-93.

8. Green, p. 98.

9. The word translated "handmaiden" in 1:48 (*doules*) also can be translated as "servant," which would highlight the parallel between Mary and Israel in this canticle. Just as Mary is the servant of the Lord (1:48), so Israel is described as the Lord's "servant" (*paidos*) in 1:54. This connection further illuminates a theme we will discuss below—how Mary can be seen in this canticle as a representative of God's people, summing up the story of Israel in her own life.

10. The Greek word used here in 1:52 to describe Israel's "low degree" (*tapeinous*) is closely related to the word used to describe Mary's "low estate" 1:48 (*tapeinosin*). As we will see, this highlights the connection between what God has done for Mary and what God will do for all his faithful people. Just as the Lord has done great things for his servant Mary in her own low estate (*tapeinosin*), so he has come to help his servant Israel and exalt all those of low degree (*tapeinous*) who are faithful to him.

11. Nolland, p. 75.

12. See J. Green, *New Testament Theology: The Theology of Luke* (Cambridge: Cambridge University Press, 1995), pp. 79-84.

Chapter Five: The Messiah's Birth

1. One difficulty with this view is that when Luke wishes to speak of an actual inn, as he does in the parable of the Good Samaritan (see Luke 10:34), he does not use the word *katalyma*. Furthermore, when Luke does use the word *katalyma*, it refers to the guest room where Jesus celebrates the Last Supper, not a commercial inn where travelers would sleep with the livestock (see 22:11).

2. B. Witherington, "The Birth of Jesus" in J. Green, et. al., eds., *Dictionary of Jesus and the Gospels* (Downers Grove, Ill.: InterVarsity Press, 1992), p. 70.

3. Green, *The Gospel of Luke*, p. 124.

4. Brown, p. 420.

Chapter Six: Pierced by a Sword

1. John Paul II, General Audience of December 11, 1996, in *Theotokos: Woman, Mother, Disciple*, p. 155

2. See Brown, p. 447.

3. In fact, in the time of Jesus, one of the major Jewish feasts, the Feast of Tabernacles, involved lighting four candelabras in the temple at night for seven days. According to some interpreters, this ritual, which illuminated the entire outer court of the temple, recalled how God's glory used to shine in the sanctuary (see Ezekiel 10:4). At the same time, it looked to the future, expressing the hope that the glory of

the Lord would soon return to Israel. See A. Edersheim, *The Temple: Its Ministry and Services* (Peabody, Mass.: Hendrickson, 1994), p. 226. On the Israelite hope for God's glory-presence to return to the temple in general, see Wright, *The New Testament and the People of God,* p. 269.

4. Brown, p. 453.

5. See Brown, pp. 270-271; Nolland, p. 35; J. McHugh, *The Mother of Jesus in the New Testament* (London: Dalton, Longman and Todd, 1975), pp. 25-27.

6. See Nolland, p. 35; McHugh, pp. 25-27.

7. S. Cunningham, *Through Many Tribulations: The Theology of Persecution in Luke-Acts* JSNT, Supp. 142 (Sheffield: Sheffield Academic Press, 1997), 47.

8. John Paul II, *Redemptoris Mater,* 16.

9. Nolland, p. 122.

10. I am grateful for this insight from a conversation with Curtis Mitch, an editor and coauthor for the *Ignatius Catholic Study Bible.*

Chapter Seven: In His Father's House

1. J. Fitzmyer, *The Gospel According to Luke I-IX* (Garden City, N.J.: Doubleday, 1981), p. 441.

2. See Green, *The Gospel of Luke*, p. 157.

3. Romano Guardini, *The Rosary of Our Lady* (Manchester, N.H.: Sophia Institute Press, 1994), pp. 94-95.

Chapter Eight: The Return of the King

1. N. Wright, *Following Jesus: Biblical Reflections on Discipleship* (Grand Rapids, Mich.: Eerdmans, 1994), p. 23.

2. N. Wright, *The New Testament and the People of God* (Minneapolis: Fortress, 1992), pp. 269-270.

3. "Nowhere in the so-called post-exilic literature is there any passage corresponding to 1 Kings 8.10f., according to which, when Solomon's temple had been finished, 'a cloud filled the house of Yahweh, so that the priests could not stand to minister because of the cloud; for the glory of YHWH, filled the house of YHWH'. Instead, Israel clung to the promises that one day the Shekinah, the glorious presence of her god, would return at last" (Wright, *The New Testament and the People of God*, p. 269). Wright goes on to cite Isaiah 52:8 and Ezekiel 43:1-2, 4-5, 7 to demonstrate the Jewish hope for God's glory-presence to return.

Chapter Nine: Silent Knight, Holy Knight

1. For a more thorough treatment, see Brown, pp. 124-129; De La Potterie, pp. 37-65.

2. One challenge to this view, however, is that it is not clear how Joseph can be described as "a just man" if he is trying to sidestep the law. To be a just man would mean he is a good, law-abiding Jew. If Joseph truly believed Mary was unfaithful and committed adultery, then as "a just man," we would expect him to be obedient to the Law and turn her in for her infidelity rather than trying to circumvent the Law.

3. Modern followers of this interpretation often support this view first by noting how the common translation of verse 18, which says Joseph was unwilling "to put her to shame," is too strong. The Greek word behind this phrase (*deigmatisai*) itself does not imply exposing shame but simply means "to show" or "to bring into the open." Since the word itself is neutral, this view holds that Joseph does not want to reveal publicly the mystery of Mary's unique motherhood. In other words, in respect for what God is doing in her life, he wants to free her from the obligation to marriage without telling everyone about her extraordinary pregnancy. See De La Potterie, pp. 41-42.

4. "The word *'almâ*, used to describe the woman, normally describes a young girl who has reached the age of puberty and is thus marriageable. It puts no stress on her virginity, although *de facto*, in the light of Israelite ethical and social

standards, most girls covered by the range of this term would be virgins" (Brown, p. 147).

5. The Septuagint Greek translation of Isaiah 7:14 specifically speaks of a virgin conceiving of this royal child.

6. See H. Waetjen, "The Genealogy as the Key to the Gospel According to Matthew," *Journal of Biblical Literature* 95 (1976), p. 226. For more on this and other parallels between the Old Testament Joseph and the New Testament Joseph, see Waetjen, pp. 225-227; S. Hahn and C. Mitch, *Ignatius Catholic Study Bible: The Gospel of Matthew* (San Francisco: Ignatius Press, 1999), p. 18; and T. Gray, "Silent Knight, Holy Knight," *Lay Witness* (December 1996), pp. 4-5, 22, which is the inspiration for this chapter title. p. 226.

7. Leo XIII, Encyclical Epistle *Quamquam pluries* (August 15, 1889) in *Leonis XIII P.M. Acta*, IX (1890), pp. 177-179. As quoted by Pope John Paul II in *Redemptoris Custos* (Boston: St. Paul Books and Media), p. 33.

Chapter Ten: The Terror of Herod

1. P. Ellis, *Matthew: His Mind and His Message* (Collegeville, Minn.: Liturgical Press, 1974), p. 27.

2. Since Jacob's name was changed to "Israel," the name "Jacob," while recalling the individual patriarch of the Book of Genesis, also is used in the Old Testament to denote the whole nation of Israel, which descended from him.

3. See, for example, a prayer from the Liturgy of the Hours for the Monday following the feast of Epiphany. "The wise men came from the East to adore the Lord in Bethlehem. Opening their treasures, they offered him three precious gifts: gold for the great King, frankincense for the true God, and myrrh for his burial, alleluia." Canticle Antiphon, Morning Prayer for Monday after Epiphany in *Christian Prayer: The Liturgy of the Hours* (New York: Catholic Book Publishing, 1976), p. 219.

4. "The word *neser*, although only occurring in Isa 11:1, became an important designation of the Messiah in the rabbinic literature and targums, and was also interpreted messianically by the Qumran community (1QH 6:15; 7:6, 8, 10, 19). Other prophets also spoke similarly of a messianic 'branch' or 'shoot,' although using different words (see Jeremiah 23:5; 33:15; Zechariah 3:8; 6:12). These words form a unified concept in looking to the fulfillment of the promises, and the mention of one doubtless brought the others to mind automatically (see STR-B 1:94). This may well be the explanation of the plural 'prophets' in Matthew's introductory formula" (D. Hagner, *Matthew 1-13* (Dallas: Word Books, 1993), p. 41).